D1552173

Herding Dogs

SELECTING AND TRAINING THE WORKING FARM DOG

By Christine Hartnagle Renna

COUNTRY DOGS™ SERIES

Kennel Club Books®
A Division of BowTie, Inc.

EDITORIAL

Andrew DePrisco *Editor-in-Chief*
Amy Deputato *Senior Editor*
Jamie Quirk *Editor*

ART

Sherise Buhagiar *Senior Graphic Artist*
Bill Jonas *Book Design*
Joanne Muzyka *Digital Imaging*

The publisher would like to thank the following photographers for their contributions to this book: Mary Bloom, Lisa Croft-Elliott, David Dalton, Tara Darling, Dale Daugherty, Isabelle Français, The Hartnagles, Robert Hoskins, Jeff Jaquish/ZingPix, Carol Ann Johnson, Alice Pantfoeder, Mary Peaslee, Dr. Robert Pollet, Christine Hartnagle Renna, Elsie Rhodes, Charlotte Schwartz, Judith Selby/SnapHappy, Stewart Event Images, Jeanne J. Taylor, Michael Trafford, Karen Ursel, and Alice van Kempen.

Cover photos by Tara Darling, Judith Selby/SnapHappy, Stewart Event Images, and Jeanne T. Taylor.

Kennel Club Books® Country Dogs™ Series

HERDING DOGS

Kennel Club Books®
A Division of BowTie, Inc.

40 Broad Street, Freehold, NJ 07728 • USA

Library of Congress Cataloging-in-Publication Data

Renna, Christine H., 1956–
Herding dogs / by Christine H. Renna.
p. cm. — (Country dog series)
ISBN 978-1-59378-737-0
1. Herding dogs. I. Title.
SF428.6.R46 2008
636.737—dc22

2008029220

Printed and bound in China

16 15 14 13 12 11 10 09   1 2 3 4 5 6 7 8 9 10

Contents

Every major agricultural nation has developed its own sheepdogs. Belgium has produced four unique sheep-herding dogs, including the solid black Groenendael, or Belgian Sheepdog.

Introduction

My passion for herding dogs led me to write this book. I have been around herding dogs all my life. My family and I value and depend on the inherent versatility and trainability of our stock dogs. In this book I share with you the history and characteristics of the different herding breeds, an interesting group of dogs that have evolved over time to handle specific situations.

These highly social working breeds have been an important part of livestock industries for centuries. They come in many shapes and sizes, colors and coats. However, you will learn that they all share the natural desire and ability to control the movement of other animals. Watching a herding dog in action is exciting and fascinating.

A herding breed can be a nice choice for a family pet, too—these dogs are loyal and intelligent and make terrific companions. They respond brilliantly to training. I grew up with herding dogs, raising and training Australian Shepherds with my family for our daily ranch work. With you I share my knowledge of and experience with the training methods we use, from the basics right up to advanced methods.

Whether you're training farms dogs or enjoying a herding companion, I have included a little something for everyone: advice on selecting the breed that will fit your personal situation as well as discussions on training, care, nutrition, and first aid.

For versatility, speed, and intelligence, no other herding dog rivals the Border Collie.

Chapter 1

The History of the Herding Dog

Herding is defined as the controlled movement of livestock from place to place by a dog under the direction of a herdsman or shepherd. The herding instinct refers to the innate craving of the dog to round up and move that livestock. Historically speaking, herders were not the dogs, but the herdsmen or sheepherders who tended the livestock. Today, stockmen and stockwomen commonly refer to their herding dogs as stockdogs, sheepdogs, or even cowdogs. People sometimes refer to herding dogs in general as working dogs.

The qualifications of a cattle dog include strength, bravery, and drive, well embodied by the rough and ready Australian Cattle Dog.

A Brief Historical Overview

Most historians agree that herding breeds are probably direct descendants of the domesticated dogs brought to Britain with sheep by Neolithic humans around 3000 BC. Dogs bred indiscriminately at first, but as early peoples settled and moved with their sheep and cattle across the British Isles, they began to selectively breed dogs that were best adapted to specific environments and herding purposes.

Between 400 BC and AD 900, the herding dogs of Celtic, Roman, Anglo-Saxon, and Viking invaders and migrants contributed to the gene pool. For example, genealogists believe some early herding dogs were introduced first to Ireland and then to Britain by Celtic people from northern Spain known as Celtiberians, during the Roman Empire. The Celtiberians called their dogs *collies*, from a Gaelic word meaning "useful." These dogs were powerful animals that were not intimidated by hard-to-control herds. They instinctively and skillfully gathered, drove, and guarded all types of livestock on the open range. Over the centuries, as European societies changed, livestock handlers further bred their herding dogs for a wide variety of characteristics and specialized skills.

Until the late nineteenth century, herding breed standards as we know them today did not exist, and a dog's lineage was very rarely recorded. Herding dogs came in all sizes, shapes, and colors, and the appearance of herding dogs was of no particular significance. The only thing that mattered was their keen working ability. It is difficult, therefore, to trace the history of herding breeds with certainty.

It is certain, however, that since medieval times shepherds, farmers, butchers, and drovers recognized and bred herding dogs to meet their individual needs. Shepherds needed even-tempered dogs capable of herding flocks on pastureland and searching for strays. Farmers and butchers who moved cattle needed quick-witted, strong dogs that could intimidate and control lively heifers on the farm or a herd driven long distances to market. Some dogs were bred to push stock; others were bred to gather and guard stock. Some were bred to keep predators away, including livestock thieves.

Differences in local terrain and climate also influenced the development of herding breeds with distinct working styles and physical characteristics. British sheep farmers along the border of England and Scotland, for example, developed herding dogs that worked silently and moved low to the ground, traits inherited from ancestors that managed herds of deer in the royal forests that once existed there. Shepherds in mountainous areas developed sure-footed dogs that

Breeds like the Australian Shepherd were developed to work on the large expanses of land in the arid climate of the American West.

could guard flocks of goats and sheep from wolves and withstand extreme cold and high altitudes. Shepherds on the Shetlands and other islands developed smaller breeds of dogs, descended from the spitzlike dogs brought there by the Vikings, that needed little food and could herd the small native sheep and ponies. Throughout history, herding dogs were expected to perform in inclement weather, on rough terrain, and against all kinds of predators. In every era, the traits for which herding dogs would become known—agility, stamina, intelligence, and hardiness—were cultivated first on the farm and then, as the livestock industry developed, on the move.

Farm Shepherds

Herding dogs on preindustrial farms shared the same keen natural instincts as the dogs used on open ranges. Typically, they received no special training. They were level-headed, unflashy dogs that made themselves useful. Often referred to as farm shepherds or farm collies, most of the old farm dogs had some type of collie background. In general, a farm shepherd was any dog connected with farm life that was used in the management of livestock. A collie was any dog that had the natural ability to control livestock, on or off the farm. Even farmers on the most modest farms who could not afford to feed several dogs required at least one good dog to gather their sheep and bring their herd of cows home.

Versatile farm dogs became known as loose-eyed, upright workers, relaxed in nature but forceful when necessary. Typically, they performed a number of routine duties. Trusted to run loose on the farm, they were responsible for bringing the cows in for milking and driving them back afterward. They gathered sheep from the pasture and searched for any animals that were lost or had strayed. When children on a farm went out into the fields among cattle or sheep that grazed in unfenced areas, the dog would remain in the field to watch over the stock while the children went off to find fun elsewhere. The farm dog also watched gates that were left open, drove out pigs that invaded the orchard and put them back in their place, and rounded up the chickens to put them away for the night. Farm dogs were often used to keep mice and rats out of the horse stables and were also good at keeping wild animals and trespassers away from their territories. They had the ability to distinguish between livestock that belonged on the farm and livestock (or possible predators) that did not belong.

The American Kennel Club Herding Group

The American Kennel Club recognizes the following breeds in its Herding Group:

Australian Cattle Dog
Australian Shepherd
Bearded Collie
Beauceron
Belgian Malinois
Belgian Sheepdog
Belgian Tervuren
Border Collie
Bouvier des Flandres
Briard
Canaan Dog
Cardigan Welsh Corgi
Collie (Rough and Smooth)
German Shepherd Dog
Old English Sheepdog
Pembroke Welsh Corgi
Polish Lowland Sheepdog
Puli
Shetland Sheepdog
Swedish Vallhund

Migration and the Livestock Industry

The development of the livestock industry played an important role in the history of herding breeds. In the days before motorized transport, droving dogs were essential to successfully move large numbers of cattle, sheep, pigs, and geese for hundreds of miles over untamed land. The life of a drover's dog was quite different from that of a sheep or farm dog. Droving dogs required stamina and the temperament to drive stubborn or anxious stock across wild countryside and through crowded towns in all kinds of weather. These invaluable dogs could accomplish the work of several stockmen. They were one of the most important assets of the shepherd or herdsman.

The British Isles have a long history of using herding dogs in trade, as Britain was once the center of a great cattle industry. It was not uncommon for a solitary drover and his pack of dogs to drive a herd of several hundred cows to market. Livestock even came to England from the far reaches of Scotland and

Catalonia's own sheepdog, the Gos d'Atura Català, is a superb herding dog, capable of handling a hundred-head flock with little difficulty.

Wales. Journeys were long and strenuous; drovers often had to swim their animals across rivers and coastal inlets, or sea lochs. Their dogs did double duty, working in packs to drive the stock by day and then guarding them at night. The movement of livestock would have been almost impossible without these hardworking and talented dogs. To this day, British stockmen use herding dogs to move livestock throughout Great Britain.

British livestock and dog breeds reached North America during the age of settlement in the seventeenth and eighteenth centuries. Settlers in the thirteen original American colonies spread out along the Atlantic coastline and took their animals with them. Their dogs inevitably bred with the dogs that accompanied settlers, traders, and adventurers from France, Spain, and elsewhere in the Americas.

Spain was known for its development of a small but hardy herding dog, toughened by exposure to and able to withstand the many hardships in the Basque region's rough, rocky, and often dangerous terrain. In the 1800s, Basque shepherds immigrated to Australia in search of opportunity, but although Australia and New Zealand became the biggest sheep producers in the world, many Basque herdsmen moved on. Along with Basques from Spain and Spanish colonies, they immigrated to the United States with their dogs and boatloads of sheep. Many were hired to care for the sheep on long ocean voyages and sometimes herd flocks on lengthy trail drives upon landing. As usual, their dogs helped manage the sheep.

The growth of the livestock industry in the United States coincided with the massive westward migration that occurred in the

1800s. Sheep and cattle ranching became big business across the central and high plains, replenished by imported sheep during periods of drought. European immigration boomed after gold was discovered in California in 1848; each wave of fortune seekers brought flocks of sheep and their own unique types of herding dogs. During the gold rush, mining camps sprang up throughout the West. Stockmen drove herds of cattle and sheep to the West to be sold to miners for meat. Herders also crossed the Great Plains on horseback, moving large numbers of cattle to northern markets and forging north–south trails that would be used for decades. Herding dogs led and followed the herds wherever they went.

One of Britain's top exports, the Border Collie stares down a wayward quartet.

Herding Breeds of Great Britain

The British, Scottish, and Welsh herding dogs so important to farmers in controlling livestock and driving sheep and goats across rugged terrain are some of the most famous dog breeds in history. Before distinct breeds were identified, different strains of black-and-white or brown herding breeds were all referred to generically as collies. Similarly, in Britain, most droving

The Belgian Tervuren moves swiftly and purposefully to move its charges.

This puppy reveals natural confidence and curiosity, which is common in herding breeds.

The Border Collie's strong-eye style sets it apart from other herding dogs; the breed was developed to neither bite nor bark.

dogs were historically known as curs (possibly from the Germanic word *cur,* meaning "to growl"). Some claim that curs were crosses between the sheepdog and the terrier. The word *cur* did not always have its present derogatory connotation; to the Welsh herdsman, the cur was a prized animal, equal in value to an ox.

Scotland, of course, is the birthplace of the ever-popular sheepdog, the Collie. The Scotch Collie descended from the Bearded Collie, one of the oldest strains of droving dogs in Great Britain. Historians believe the Bearded Collie developed from a pair of Polish Lowland Sheepdogs brought to Scotland by Polish traders in 1514. Their hardy descendants were able to herd independently without commands from their masters. Stockmen developed a close working partnership with these dogs based on cooperation, affection, and respect.

Through selective breeding, stockmen set out to produce and improve specific valuable traits in their herding dogs. Hunting dogs such as pointers and setters were bred with herding dogs to provide a "good nose" and a "strong eye."

The Whippet's fleet foot and quiet nature added swiftness to the mix. Eventually, crossbreeding produced superior athletic ability, light and quick movement, and a canny livestock sense. Many of the early herding breeds had temperaments sensitive to a handler's will yet independent enough to work without constant direction from their masters.

In 1894, on the English–Scottish border, it is said that Adam Tefler introduced the first of what would become the modern Border Collie, the breed that most closely resembles the old-time collie of Scotland. Today, the Border Collie is recognized the world over as the most stylish of herding breeds, able to control herds of sheep with calm precision, lightning-quick reflexes, and an uncommon intelligence.

The Border Collie was bred to work calmly and swiftly without barking or nipping (Whippet influence). Its intense gaze or "eye" (Pointer-Setter influence) alone is capable of intimidating sheep and making them obey. Border Collies were also bred to face the sheep head-on with their belly and shoulders close to the ground, enhancing the intimidation factor by imitating the stance of a predator. The Border Collie contributed to the heritage of many other breeds around the world, including the Ovelheiro Gaúcho, a sheepdog originally developed in Brazil.

Welsh Sheepdogs were among the early herding breeds, used to drive large flocks of sheep and herds of cattle to English markets. Old manuscripts describe ancestors of the modern Welsh Sheepdog as dogs that guarded the stock. The early Welsh farm dogs protected their owners and animals from rustlers and wild animals in addition to performing their herding duties. Bred for general farmwork, they were described as good watchdogs that barked at intruders but were gentle with children.

Other British herding breeds such as the short-legged Welsh Corgis (Cardigan and Pembroke) were developed to drive cattle and nip at the heels of stragglers. Corgis worked stock by forming a semicircle behind the herd instead of moving along the sides like a sheepdog. First introduced to the lands they are associated with by the Celts in about 1200 BC, the Corgis' most useful era was hundreds of years ago, when all land was owned

The Bearded Collie pre-dates the more popular Collie of Scotland and likely developed from the Polski Owczarek Nizinny (PON), or Polish Lowland Sheepdog.

by the Crown. Tenant farmers called *crofters* were allowed to fence off only a few acres around their dooryards. Cattle were grazed on unfenced common lands, and the best grazing places were highly sought after. The Cardigan was trained to drive his own cattle to a good spot at the direction of the farmer and to watch over the cattle while they grazed. He also chased any neighboring cattle that invaded his herd's space by nipping at their heels, always anticipating and swiftly dodging the ensuing bovine kick.

Old English Sheepdogs are thought to have been developed by British stockmen from the early types of Bearded Collie and Russian Ovcharka to handle sheep and cattle in more rugged terrain. They were popular with farmers who needed an agile dog to take their cattle and sheep to market. Sometimes called Bobtails, Old English Sheepdogs were customarily docked or bobbed, as were most herding breeds in the eighteenth century. In Britain, the docking of tails exempted a farmer or drover from paying taxes on his working dogs. Although this exemption was discontinued, docking is still practiced on many breeds, especially sporting breeds. Today, docking and ear cropping have been outlawed throughout most of Europe, however, and it is becoming increasingly common to see Bobtails with tails on streets and farms as well as in show rings.

Drovers employed by the Smithfield meat markets outside London used assertive cowdogs, known as Smithfields, that would urge stock forward with their bark and bite. Historical records depict Smithfields as large, stockily built, black bobtail shepherds or Collies, reflecting the influence of the herding dogs that accompanied the Romans. Old English Sheepdogs and Sussex Sheepdogs were also acknowledged as Smithfields.

Shetland Sheepdogs were indigenous to the Shetland Islands, between Scotland and Norway where the Atlantic meets the North Sea. They acquired the name *Toonie* because they herded the ponies off the "toons" (towns). Their heritage probably can be traced to the Middle Ages, when Scotland occupied and eventually won control of the Shetlands from Norway. The islands' small Nordic herding dogs were at some point likely crossed with ancestors of the Border Collie that accompanied sheep imported to the Shetlands from Scotland, producing a breed that resembles a small Border Collie.

The English Shepherd, known as the quintessential versatile farm dog in early America, descended

The Old English Sheepdog is closely related to the Bearded Collie, from which it likely derived. Both have similar coats and working styles.

Like the larger Collie, its unmistakable cousin the Shetland Sheepdog hails from Scotland and was used to herd sheep and perhaps ponies.

A working breed from North America despite its name, the English Shepherd is a composite of various collie-type dogs from the United Kingdom.

from collies that themselves were descendants of dogs introduced to the British Isles in the Roman invasion of 55 BC. They were natural guard dogs that watched over the master's family as well as the flock. Equally even-tempered around children and adults, they were expected to protect children at play, bark to alert the family when a stranger approached, and position themselves between the children and the approaching stranger. In addition to performing their herding duties, they hunted small game and kept the barn free from vermin.

Although they are not considered herding breeds in the traditional sense, Kerry Blue Terriers, Soft Coated Wheaten Terriers, and several others terriers are multitalented all-purpose farm dogs and family companions. Years ago they were depended on as herding, guarding, hunting, retrieving, and vermin-destroying workers. They were equally trusted to watch over the children and curl up at the hearth. A variety of dog groups, including hounds, were crossed to obtain these traits; it is likely, for instance, that a fair amount of Irish Wolfhound blood ended up in the terriers.

Herding Breeds of Continental Europe

In the pastoral zones of continental Europe, herding dogs were used daily to move animals (sheep, goats, cattle, geese) from the farm to unfenced grazing fields and then back to the farm to be housed or stabled in a barn at night. Because shepherds were frequently hired to care for several herds or flocks belonging to different owners, the continental breeds were developed to handle large groups of animals. In addition, because seasonal migration

Seasonal migration is a way of life for shepherds in some European countries. This transhumance was photographed in Catalonia and was guided by a single Gos d'Atura Català and his master.

The Belgian Sheepdog, or Groenendael, represents the longhaired, solid black breed of continental shepherd from Belgium.

(transhumance) between summer and winter pastures was practiced throughout Europe—especially in mountainous areas and parts of eastern Europe—dogs with keen guardian instincts were needed to keep predators away.

Consequently, the continental breeds tend to be more protective than some of the other breeds are. They have a strong work ethic and are weather-resistant, highly adaptable, hardy, and long-lived. An example of this type of mountain sheepdog is the Spotted Tiger, which has been shepherding large flocks for hundreds of years. Spotted Tigers were bred to nip at cows' heels and duck down low to avoid being kicked, a working style much like that of the Welsh Corgi. They were also adept at moving large herds of cows along roads without fences and keeping them under control to prevent their charges from grazing crops in adjacent fields.

Herding practices in the mountains have changed very little over the centuries, although transhumance is now more often accomplished by motorized transport than on foot. A few shepherds still make the journey on foot as they have done for countless generations and continue to utilize agile, quick-thinking herding dogs to maneuver the flocks and herds on such long and difficult journeys.

Other continental breeds include four varieties of the Belgian Sheepdog: the longhaired Tervuren and Groenendael, the shorthaired Malinois, and—rarest of these breeds—the wirehaired Laekenois. Until the latter part of the nineteenth century, all four were working sheepdogs and guard dogs. As the twentieth century approached, mechanized transport was developed and improved, and the services of these dogs were no longer required. Nowadays, the Tervuren and Groenendael, both popular breeds in Belgium, work for the police and the military as guard dogs. In Holland, Dutch Shepherds, quite similar to Belgian Sheepdogs, also prove to be multitalented working dogs that can be seen in all three coat types.

Developed as a cattle drover, the Giant Schnauzer derives from working dogs from southern Germany. Some were crossed with Great Danes to produce dogs large and bold enough to move livestock to market centers near Munich. After modern transportation methods replaced cattle drives in Germany, the Giant Schnauzer was used as a butcher's dog and was often employed as a stockyard helper or brewery guard.

Bouvier (meaning "cowherder" or "ox drover") dogs were used in Belgium and France for working large livestock. The popular Bouvier des Flandres and the very rare Bouvier de Ardennes are two examples of cowdogs able to drive and protect very large herds.

The Bouvier des Flandres is a solid, four-square cowherder from Belgium, popular throughout Europe and America.

Cowdogs, or Sennenhunds as they're known in Switzerland, represent four of that nation's most handsome breeds—the Appenzeller, Entlebucher, Bernese Mountain Dog, and Greater Swiss Mountain Dog. The Bernese and "Swissy" are more popular in America and abroad. The Appenzeller and the Entlebucher are considerably smaller than their two larger cousins but are heavy-boned and muscular, making them efficient at pulling carts and wagons. The rarest of the four, the Appenzeller, is said to be either a native breed dating to the Bronze Age or a

Well insulated from the cold, the Puli has a corded coat that sets him apart from every other continental herding dog.

molosser descendant brought to Switzerland by the Romans. Entlebuchers are the smallest of the Sennenhunds, used as watchdogs after being introduced to the Roman nobility. They were brought into Switzerland and used primarily by Alpine herdsman to drive cattle. Bernese Mountain Dogs were used as cattle dogs and draft dogs. Their ancestors were most likely large mastiff-type dogs, but dogs left as guardians at Roman outposts were also crossed with local herding dogs, resulting in the Bernese Mountain Dogs that we know today. The Greater Swiss Mountain Dog is the largest and perhaps the oldest of the four Swiss varieties, bred from the mastiff types left behind by the Roman armies and used for herding and draft work.

Smaller, multipurpose herding dogs, the Pumi and the Puli arrived in Hungary with the Magyars about a thousand years ago. They worked outdoors on the vast Hungarian plains, herding and guarding the flocks in all kinds of weather. It was not uncommon for the shepherd and his dogs to stay out in the fields day and night even during winter months, and the Puli's corded coat helped insulate him against extreme weather conditions.

Also from Hungary, the Mudi is a rare herding dog that suffered near extinction at the end of World War II. Known as the Driver Dog by some shepherds, the Mudi may have come into existence in the eighteenth or nineteenth century when Hungarian herding dogs were crossed with various prick-eared German herding dogs. The Mudi is a versatile farm dog that has been used mainly for herding cattle, sheep, and pigs and occasionally as a working terrier and hunting dog. The Mudi adapts well to different climates, working conditions, and situations.

Two breeds of herding dog developed in the Pyrenees, mountain ranges that stretch roughly west to east at the border of France and Spain. The Catalonian or Catalan Sheepdog, known as Gos d'Atura Català in Spain, has shepherded flocks in this region for centuries. The Pyrenean Shepherd, known as Berger des Pyrenees in France, also has a long history as a herding breed able to work large flocks.

Nordic Herding Breeds

The influence of Nordic sled dogs on herding dogs is evident in the anatomy and coats of many of Northern Europe's purebred dogs. The most popular example of the Nordic herding dog is the snow-white Samoyed, a member of the spitz family of North Russia and Siberia. Samoyeds have long been treasured for their versatility as watchdogs, companions, sled dogs, and reindeer herders. They were bred by nomadic Samoyed tribes in northeast Siberia.

From Norway, the Norwegian Buhund (or Norwegian Sheepdog) is a herder as well as a guardian and is

The petite Pyrenean Sheepdog, or Berger des Pyrenees, works closely with the more popular white giant, the Great Pyrenees, in the mountainous regions of France.

The Swedish Vallhund is a fast-thinking, swift-moving cowherder.

a member of the spitz family known in Scandinavia even before the days of the Vikings. Icelandic Sheepdogs are thought to be descendants of the smaller herding dogs brought to Iceland during the time of colonization by the Vikings.

Finland and Sweden have their own versions of the Lapphund, believed to be the original native dogs used by the Lapps to hunt reindeer in Lapland and evolved from hunter to herder. Swedish Lapphunds, Lapponian Herders, and Finnish Lapphunds were developed from the ancient Arctic spitz dogs of Siberian dwellers.

Another Swedish example is the Swedish Vallhund or Vastgotaspet, named for the province of Vastgotaspet in southwestern Sweden. There are similarities between the Vallhund and the Welsh Corgi in appearance and also in their working characteristics. The Vallhund is believed to have been used by the Vikings and then brought to the British Isles. It is also possible that a Corgi-type dog was imported to Sweden as long ago as the eleventh century. Vallhunds have long been valued as cattle herders with the instinct to nip at the hocks of a slow-moving cow to prod it along.

Herding Breeds from Down Under

There is no doubt that sheep breeding in Australia has long been one of the continent's most valuable industries. Australian farmers needed working dogs that were suited to an unforgiving climate and inhospitable farming conditions. Many Australian dog breeds were developed by crossing German and British collies with British Smithfields, which had full rough coats like Beardies or Pyrenean Shepherds. They were unable to cope with the Australian heat and notoriously barked too much. Sometime around the 1830s, black bobtailed Smithfields were crossed with the Australian native dog, the

Dingo, resulting in bobtailed dogs called Timmins Biters.

The pride of the Australian dog world, the Kelpie was developed and widely used by the Australian sheep-farming community. The Kelpie descended from British stock to work cattle and sheep. Its working style and intensity is similar to that of the Border Collie. A unique feature of the Kelpie is its ability to herd sheep in stock pens and loading chutes by "backing," running over the backs of tightly packed sheep to the front of the flock and pushing them up the chute or to the gate.

The first settlers in sparsely populated colonial Australia set out to create a breed of dog that could muster and move wild cattle. The principal requirements of this breed of dog were strength, great stamina, and the ability and willingness to bite. Australian Cattle Dogs, known as Queensland Blue Heelers, were successfully developed for this kind of cattle work. The Australian Cattle Dog primarily derived from a mix of smooth blue-speckled Collie imports from Scotland and wild Australian Dingoes. Australian Kelpie, Dalmatian, and Bull Terrier lines were also added. The result was an excellent herding dog, with few equals, who worked the stock quietly yet forcefully, willing and able to drive cattle across vast distances under harsh, hot, and dusty conditions.

Koolies, once known as German Koolies, were originally thought to be descended from blue merle dogs of Scottish border ancestry and Smithfields. It is generally believed that these dogs

The Australian Kelpie ranks as the world's most hard-core herding dog—untiring, tough, and all business.

The German Shepherd Dog is respected and admired throughout the world for its versatility, intelligence, and loyalty.

probably were crossed to Tiger dogs, a strain of old German Shepherds imported from Germany to Australia by European immigrant farmers with their Saxony Merino sheep in the 1800s. They have also been reported to have been bred from a variety of Welsh sheepdogs known as Welsh Heelers. Most likely, both breeds contributed to the formation of Australian Koolies, one of Australia's oldest breeds.

Collies were used for quiet and careful work in close quarters at lambing time. The New Zealand Sheepdogs, or Huntaways, were used to force massive flocks of sheep into sheep yards and to find sheep out in the steep hills. They were named after the Huntaway sheepherding competitions.

Herding Dogs in the United States

It has been said that the southern Appalachian ranges of Kentucky and Tennessee could not have been settled without the pioneers' "curs," or bear dogs, of which there are a number of recognized breeds and varieties today. The Blue Lacy or Texas Blue Lacy, the Kemmer Cur, the Leopard Cur, the Mountain Cur, the Southern Black Mouth Cur, and the Yellow Black Mouth Cur are among the different types of cur dogs; these are herding dogs that are also able to hunt big and small game. Curs are not afraid of bears or wild cats and have been known to fight both.

With a fierce love of the hunt, the high-energy Mountain Curs have been used on raccoons, mountain lions, wild hogs, and other game. The Southern Black Mouth Cur and Yellow Black Mouth Cur are very similar in looks and coloration and are said to be the model for the canine hero of Fred Gibson's classic novel *Old Yeller*. These two cur dogs are believed to be descendants of some type of hound crossed with a mastiff. Black Mouth Curs of both varieties have made topnotch cowdogs and hogdogs for generations.

In parts of the United States, Louisiana Catahoula Leopard Dogs and several other cur breeds were developed to hunt or tree larger game, particularly wild hogs, which can be fiercely aggressive. Catahoula Leopards, the spotted dogs affectionately referred to as "Cats," were brought to the American South by sixteenth-century Spanish explorers in their quest for gold and established themselves in Louisiana's Catahoula Lake area. There is some speculation that their genetic makeup includes red wolf. For generations, this breed too has been referred to as cowdogs or hogdogs. Catahoulas work better in packs or pairs; on a wild hog hunt, one dog distracts its prey and the other goes for a catch.

In competition, some of the earliest trials developed for these dogs included catch-and-mark contests, in which the handler and dogs catch and mark a wild hog.

Other breeds of herding dogs developed in the United States include the ever-popular Australian Shepherd, the versatile farm dog known as the English Shepherd, and the curlike Blue Lacy.

Herding dogs attend to a variety of livestock, from sheep and goats to cows and beyond, on many different terrains and in all kinds of weather and climates.

Chapter

2

The Modern Herding Dog

Modern herding dogs work on farms, live in rural homes, and are kept as family pets in the city. There are enough variations between the breeds to provide a suitable dog for most situations. Today's herding dog is not merely a herder or a drover. He is a versatile and intelligent herder that can adapt to changing circumstances in the modern world around him.

Today's Farm and Livestock Dogs

Farmers and ranchers make their living off the land and from the stock they raise. Today, as in all ages in all places, they attend to

Breeds like the Australian Kelpie are capable of handling large, unruly livestock like cows and bulls.

watering, feeding, and caring for their animals. At certain times of the year they breed, shear, brand, and attend the birthing of their animals. They rise early, work long hours, and rarely have days off. They work outdoors in all weather conditions. And as always, their faithful dogs are at their side.

The farm dog remains a companion, a guardian, and a hard worker that can be counted on to do the job at hand. Farmers and ranchers still use herding dogs for many livestock-control purposes. Typical responsibilities of the modern herding dog include gathering and moving livestock and keeping the flock out of harm's way. Herding dogs on modern farms can watch over livestock while the farmer attends to chores such as repairing a fence, watering livestock, or cleaning a barn. The herding dog's jobs are chiefly physical, and the dogs are expected to do whatever the farmer or rancher requires according to the situation.

Nevertheless, since the advent of modern industrialized agriculture, machinery does a lot of farmwork once done by hand. The droving duties of modern livestock-herding dogs are few, as livestock is mainly transported by vehicles, not on hoof. More herding breed dogs live off farms and ranches than on. Nowadays, few of these breeds have full-time jobs. Their inbred or instinctive desire to herd livestock remains strong, though. Most herding dogs need outlets in which they can do what they were bred to do. Without a way to burn off excess energy, herding dogs can become hyperactive and destructive, often to the point of becoming a nuisance. Your knowledge of the following herding breeds is incomplete if you overlook their need for regular, strenuous exercise.

The Herding Breeds

The herding breeds have in common a natural skill and desire to control the movements of other animals, most often sheep and cattle. They accomplish this by stalking and staring, by barking and by nipping, depending on the breed. Some have gathering tendencies, whereas others have driving tendencies. Herding breeds come from around the world. The following breeds are known primarily as herding dogs, though there are other breeds capable of herding that are not included in this chapter.

Border Collies respond to the shepherd's vocal commands and training-stick gestures.

Hailing from Switzerland, the Appenzeller is a stellar cattle drover and property guard.

Appenzell Cattle Dog (Appenzeller Sennenhund)

The Appenzeller Sennenhund is a muscular working dog, prized for its intelligence and ability to learn a variety of tasks quickly. Sometimes used as watchdogs, Appenzellers get along well with livestock and other animals. Like their more common cousins, the Bernese Mountain Dogs, they are great companions that love the outdoors, although they do not adapt very well as indoor house pets because they thrive on running free. They are energetic, powerful, athletic, outgoing, and confident around familiar people but reserved toward strangers.

It is a medium-size breed; males range in height from nineteen to twenty-four inches and females are slightly smaller, from eighteen to twenty inches. Males weigh between fifty-five and seventy pounds; females, slightly less. Appenzeller Sennenhunds have short double coats that are smooth, thick, and glossy. Their coat is easy to care for and striking in color. Like all of the other Swiss mountain dog breeds, the traditional colors are black with white and rust markings.

Australian Cattle Dog (Blue Heeler, Queensland Heeler, Queensland Blue Heeler, and Queensland Red Heeler)

The Australian Cattle Dog is a courageous, tough, intelligent working dog with strength and endurance unsurpassed by any other dog of its size. It is very athletic, willing and able to drive cattle across vast distances under harsh, hot, and dusty conditions, and thus well suited for the climate of Queensland. It is one of the more dominant herding breeds. The Australian Cattle Dog must be treated firmly but fairly, and may require a dominant owner. It is typically reserved with strangers and fiercely protective when it perceives its property or master as being threatened. It is often described as hardheaded and stubborn.

Australian Cattle Dogs are medium-size muscular dogs that stand seventeen to twenty inches. Males usually weigh between twenty-one and forty-four pounds; females, slightly less. Their double coat is either blue or red speckled with or without white markings. The outercoat is smooth and straight, which protects them from the elements, and the short but dense undercoat resists rain.

Tough in body and mind, the Australian Cattle Dog excels on large, rugged livestock but may be too intense for poultry or young sheep or goats.

Australian Kelpie

This breed is known as a rugged, tireless, well-rounded sheepdog. A true all-around stockdog, the Australian Kelpie is favored in the Outback because it is capable of working all day even in intense heat.

Kelpies are medium-size dogs measuring from seventeen to twenty inches high at the shoulder and weighing from twenty-five to forty-five pounds. They have a short double coat, consisting of a smooth short outercoat and dense undercoat. They are seen in a

Possessing a one-track mind, the Australian Kelpie lives to work.

variety of colors: black and tan, red, red and tan, fawn, chocolate, and smoke blue. Their all-weather coat allows them to live in either hot or cold temperatures.

Australian Koolie (German Coolie or Coulie)

The eye-catching Koolie looks like a cross between a Border Collie, a Kelpie, and an Australian Cattle Dog, displaying traits of all three breeds. They are happy dogs, loyal and devoted to their families. Australian Koolies are medium-size dogs ranging from seventeen to twenty-two inches in height and weighing twenty-eight to forty-eight pounds. Predominantly red merle and blue merle, Koolies also come in solid colors.

Perhaps the most beautiful of all herding dogs is the Australian Shepherd, although the author may be somewhat biased!

Australian Shepherd

This breed is not registered in Australia as a native breed. They are believed to have originated in the Basque region of the Pyrenees Mountains between Spain and France. The actual origin of the Australian Shepherd cannot be traced through records, as the Basques had no written language. However, the dogs we refer to as Australian Shepherds accompanied Basque herders from Australia to the United States in the 1800s. Although there are many theories about its origin, the breed as we know it today developed exclusively in the United States.

The Australian Shepherd is quick, agile, attentive, and animated. It is an intelligent, active dog with an even disposition. Although good-natured, it is somewhat reserved at initial meetings. Very protective of their family members, Aussies make good pets. They are also strong and muscular and thus capable of doing a full day's work.

The general appearance of the Australian Shepherd is that of a well-balanced dog of medium size and bone. Males range between twenty and twenty-three inches in height; females, between eighteen and twenty-one inches. Males weigh fifty to sixty-five pounds and females between forty and fifty-five pounds.

The Australian Shepherd's coat comes in many beautiful combinations of colors such as blue merle or red merle, or either solid black or solid red (sometimes referred to as liver). All colors can be accented with white and/or copper points. Their medium-length hair is of medium texture, straight to slightly wavy, and weather resistant. The downy soft undercoat varies in quantity depending on climate. Hair is short and smooth on the head, ears, front of the forelegs, and below the hocks. Backs of forelegs and britches are feathered. There is a moderate mane and frill, more pronounced in dogs than in bitches.

A smaller version of the breed, known as the Miniature Australian Shepherd, has been gaining in popularity as a pet. It offers all of the appealing personality traits of the Aussie in a smaller package.

From the Azores, west of Portugal, the Azores Cattle Dog remains one of the rarest herding dogs in the world.

Azores Cattle Dog (Cão de Fila de São Miguel)

In Portugal, the Azores Cattle Dog is also known as the Cão de Fila de São Miguel. Not yet well known in North America, it comes from the remote Azores island group, Portuguese possessions in the eastern North Atlantic Ocean, where it has been used only for working purposes. This cattle dog can be either aggressive or docile, depending on the breeder and the dog's bloodlines. The Azores's forceful working style makes it a dog capable of dominating and manipulating even the worst-tempered animals.

Males range from twenty to twenty-four inches in height; females, from nineteen to twenty-three inches. Males weigh fifty-five to seventy-seven pounds and females weigh forty-four to sixty-six pounds. Their coat is short, smooth, and dense with a strong texture. They come in colors from yellow to fawn to gray, in light or dark shades.

Bearded Collie

The Bearded Collie was developed in the inhospitable climatic conditions and terrain of the Scottish Highlands. Capable of working independent of commands, it is highly trainable, exhibiting varying degrees of eye. Beardies are upright workers, and some use barking to flush out stock. They have a lovable personality—joyful, affectionate, happy-go-lucky, and playful.

Beardies are twenty to twenty-two inches in height and weigh forty to sixty pounds. They are shaggy all over, even under the chin (hence their name!). They sport a long double coat with a soft, furry undercoat that fits close to the skin. They have a short muzzle, broad skull, and large teeth. The Beardie carries its long tail down low and wags it high when excited.

Beauceron (French Short-haired Shepherd, Beauce Shepherd, Berger de Beauce, and Bas Rouge)

Along with its cousin the Briard, the Beauceron is among the largest herding breeds of France. In the early nineteenth century, the longhaired Briard and the shorthaired Beauceron were considered to be two different varieties of the same breed. In 1896, each was officially recognized as a distinct breed. Both breeds are competent sheepdogs and guard dogs. Like other European herding breeds, they are capable of managing large flocks. They need little or no assistance from their flock masters when used to guard sheep and cattle.

Their temperament is self-assured, never mean or timid. They are gentle but fearless. This breed is extremely versatile and is an ideal pet and strong working dog.

Males range from twenty-five to twenty-seven inches in height; females, from twenty-four to twenty-six inches. The Beauceron is a medium-size, powerful, well-built, muscular dog. The outercoat is coarse and dense. The undercoat is short, fine, dense, and downy, mouse gray in color; it does not show through the outercoat.

Belgian Laekenois

The least common of the four Belgian Sheepdog breeds, the rough-haired Laekenois is a very intelligent breed. The Belgian Laekenois is a sturdy, well-proportioned, medium-size dog with a wire coat. The coat, described as rough, dry, and tousled, is noticeably the same length all over. The height on average is twenty-four inches for males and twenty-three inches for females.

The ears are small, triangular, and set high on the head. Eyes are brown, average in size, and slightly almond-shaped, while the muzzle is of equal length to the topskull and somewhat pointed. The nose is black and the tail is very long.

The wirehaired Belgian sheepdog known as the Laekenois is the least known of the four Belgian breeds.

Belgian Malinois

The temperament of the Belgian Malinois, one of the four Belgian Sheepdog breeds, is confident. This breed exhibits neither shyness nor aggressiveness. The Belgian Malinois's height is often evenly proportioned to its length. It has an elegant appearance and is known to carry itself quite proudly, with its high-held head, muscular build, and flowing gait. Males are from twenty-four to twenty-six inches in height and females are around twenty-two to

The Belgian Malinois excels in many areas, from sheep-herding and flock protection to police work and border control.

The majestic Groenendael is fast becoming a favorite working dog worldwide.

twenty-four inches in height. The coat is short, straight, and hard enough to be weather-resistant, with a dense undercoat.

Belgian Sheepdog (Groenendael)

The Belgian Sheepdog is the solid black herder known as the Groenendael, named after the Belgian village where the breed was developed. The Belgian Sheepdog remains the most popular of the four Belgian herding dogs, known collectively in the United Kingdom as Belgian Shepherds. The four breeds—Groenendael, Malinois, Tervuren, and Laekenois—are anatomically alike and vary only in coat color, length, and texture.

Males are twenty-four to twenty-six inches in height; females, twenty-two to twenty-four inches. The AKC breed standard for the Belgian Sheepdog describes a dense undercoat and an outercoat that is long, straight, and abundant, with a texture of medium harshness (neither silky nor wiry). The breed's long coat is not as long as that of a Bearded Collie or Polish Lowland Sheepdog. Belgian Sheepdogs adapt well to extreme temperatures.

Belgian Tervuren

The Belgian Tervuren's attitude toward humans is observant but not apprehensive. This Belgian breed is affectionate, friendly, and even possessive toward family members. The ideal height for a male is twenty-four to twenty-six inches and for a female is twenty-two to twenty-four inches. The Tervuren's coat is similar to that of the Groenendael, but instead of being solid black, it is rich fawn to russet mahogany with black overlay. Like the other three Belgian breeds, it adapts well to extreme temperatures and conditions.

Bergamasco

Historically, the shaggy Bergamasco watched over flocks of sheep in the Alps of northern Italy. Like most other herding breeds, the Bergamasco is loyal and protective of family members but reserved with strangers. It is a highly energetic and agile dog, patient, tolerant, and attentive.

The Bergamasco is a square-bodied, medium-size dog with a thick, distinctive coat that forms cords, sometimes called flocks, that start at the spine and eventually reach the ground. Females average twenty-two inches in height; males, around twenty-four inches. Average weight is fifty-eight to eighty-four pounds for males and fifty-seven to seventy-one pounds for females.

The Bergamasco's thick coat (considered hair, not fur) protects it

A trio of Belgian Tervurens illustrates this breed's natural beauty and robust construction.

The unique Bergamasco possesses a coat that creates cords or flocks. Puppies are born soft and shaggy.

against all kinds of weather. Its matted hair also drapes over its eyes, which protects them from damage by sunlight reflecting off snow. Despite its matted appearance, the coat requires very little care except for occasional brushing and bathing. The Bergamasco Sheepdog is best suited for seasonal to very cold climates.

Border Collie

The Border Collie is known as the world's premiere sheepherding dog. Its agility, athleticism, and stamina are equaled by its grace and substance. Its hard, muscular body is well balanced, conveying the impression of effortless movement and endless endurance. Border Collies are extremely intelligent, regarded by many as the smartest dog on earth. Their keen, alert expression, eagerness, and intensity are key characteristics of the breed.

Border Collies have the ability to sprint wide to gather groups of sheep from great distances. They respond exceptionally well to whistle commands, often from as far as a mile away. Willing to work with another dog without argument, most

The unmistakable Border Collie can come in almost any color, including this attractive tricolor. Color is mostly immaterial to the dog's abilities.

Rough and rugged, the Bouvier des Flandres is built for cow duty.

Border Collies will work for anyone who can give them the commands (verbal, hand signal, or whistle) that they have learned in their basic training. Border Collies are trained to respond instantly to the handler's orders. They are independent dogs but when trained will move the stock in any direction the handler commands.

The Border Collie is not a breed for everyone: such an exceedingly smart dog must be kept busy. Unless you can spend lots of time playing Frisbee or fetch, find someone with agility equipment you can use, or teach the dog to herd sheep or ducks, forget the Border Collie. This dog doesn't just need exercise; it needs meaningful exercise and lots of it. A walk won't do unless it gets to fetch something, herd something, or climb over, under, around, or through something.

The Border Collie is a medium-size breed. Males range from nineteen to twenty-two inches in height; females, from eighteen to twenty-one inches in height. Males weigh thirty to forty-five pounds; females, twenty-seven to forty-two pounds.

Border Collies come in two coat types, rough and smooth. Both have a close-fitting, dense, weather-resistant double coat with a soft undercoat. The outer layer of the rough coat is moderately long with a medium texture, never wiry or silky. The smooth coat has a coarser feel and is short all over.

Bouvier des Flandres (Flanders Cattle Dog and Vlaanse Koehond)

The Bouvier des Flandres is powerfully built, rugged, and formidable in appearance. The Bouvier is agile, spirited, and bold with a calm and steady manner. It needs plenty of room to exercise but is not an outdoor dog. Its obedient and pleasant nature make it an ideal companion for a loving person or family.

Males range in size from twenty-four to twenty-seven inches; females, from twenty-two to twenty-six inches. The males weigh seventy to ninety pounds; females, sixty to eighty pounds.

This breed has a double coat. The outercoat is shaggy, rough, and harsh and requires lots of attention.

Briard (Chien Berger de Brie)

This breed is used for guarding and herding stock in France. It is an "all-rounder" that is up to any task. The Briard is a bighearted, gentle, and loving dog that makes a wonderful family pet and excellent watchdog.

Males range from twenty-four to twenty-seven inches in height; females, from twenty-two to twenty-five inches. Male and female weigh on average around seventy-five pounds.

The Briard's coat is described as coarse, hard, and dry (making a rasping sound between the fingers). It lies flat, falling naturally in long, slightly wavy locks with the sheen of good health. The undercoat is fine

The versatile Briard proves a reliable farm dog, family companion, and all-around herder.

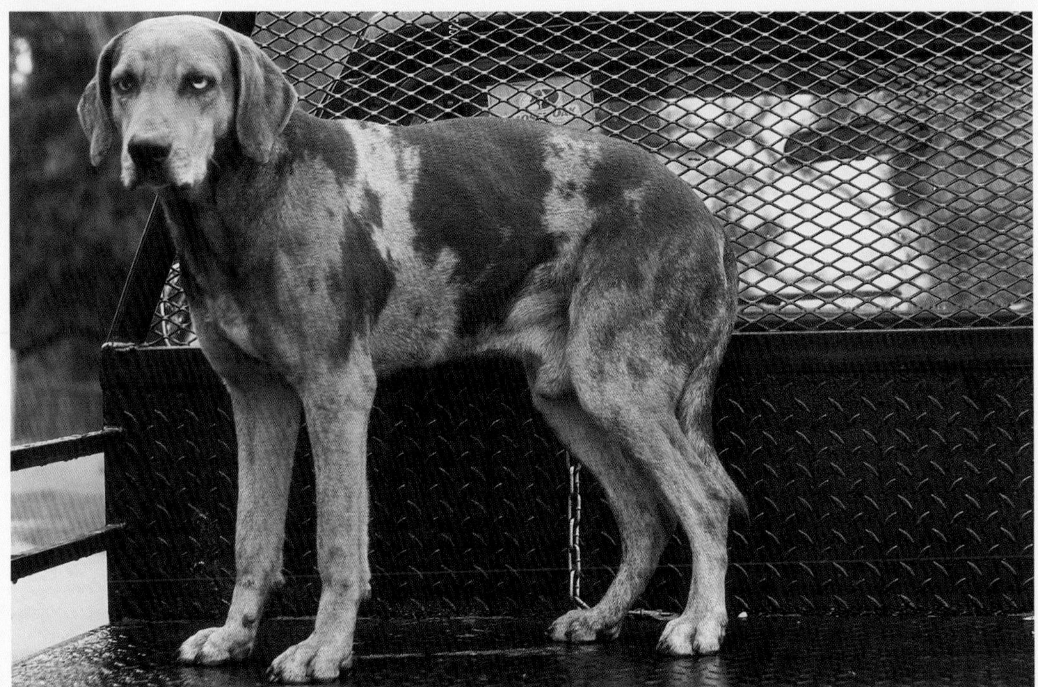

Hound dog through and through, the Catahoula Leopard Dog can herd almost as well as he can hunt.

and tight all over the body. The coat repels dirt and water and will become matted without regular grooming.

Canaan Dog (Kelev K'naani)

The essential characteristics of Israel's Canaan Dog are those which have enabled it to survive for centuries in the desert. The Canaan Dog is able to stand up to jackals, hyenas, and wolves. It is intelligent and adapts well to a wide range of temperatures and circumstances. It has a strong sense of territoriality and is extremely defensive but not naturally aggressive. Its first reaction, when confronted by an intruder, is not to attack but to stay out of reach and bark continuously.

The Canaan Dog is a medium-size, well-balanced, strong, and square dog with a wedge-shaped head and erect low-set ears. It stands from nineteen to twenty-four inches in height and weighs between thirty-five and fifty-five pounds. It has a dense double coat with a straight, harsh outercoat that is between a half-inch and one and one-half inches long. The undercoat is dense but short and close to the body.

Catahoula Leopard Dog

Hailing from the state of Louisiana, the Catahoula Leopard Dog, also known as the Catahoula Hog Dog, Catahoula Cur, or Catahoula Hound, is independent, protective, and territorial. It is affectionate toward family members and needs human attention, direction, and training.

Catahoula Leopard Dogs are medium to large dogs with drooping ears, friendly yet sturdy faces, and webbed feet. The males weigh from fifty-five to eighty pounds and are twenty-two to twenty-six inches in height. Females average twenty to twenty-four inches in height. They have a single coat that is short and tight, and they need to be kept warm in really cold weather.

Catalonian Sheepdog (Catalonian Shepherd, Gos d'Atura Català, and Perro de Pastor Catalán)

The Catalonian Sheepdog is a rare breed that originated in Catalonia, the northeast corner of Spain, as a sheep guard and farm dog. This breed tolerates heat, cold, and all kinds of weather. It is hearty and pleasant in character and devoted to the shepherd and the flocks entrusted to it. Its vigilance and wariness of strangers can at times make it appear unsociable.

The breed ranges from eighteen to twenty-two inches in height and weighs around forty pounds. Its coat is long and either flat or slightly wavy, ranging in color from fawn to dark sable and light to dark gray. There is a shorthaired version of this breed, but it is nearly extinct.

The small but sturdy Catalonian Sheepdog is herder *numero uno* in his homeland.

The ever-popular Collie, in the familiar rough coat, makes an ideal family companion.

The Dutch Shepherd, shown here in the long coat, is a multipurpose herding dog from Holland.

COLLIE

There are two varieties of Collie, Smooth and Rough; the latter is by far the more common. Collies are noble, sweet dogs that are easy to train and loyal family members devoted to loved ones.

Both varieties are medium-size dogs. The females range from twenty-two to twenty-four inches in height; the males range from twenty-four to twenty-six inches.

The Smooth Collie has a short, dense, flat coat. The Rough Collie has a long outercoat that is abundant except on the head and legs. This coat is straight and harsh-textured. The furry undercoat is soft and thick, protecting the dog in wet weather.

CUR

Several types of dogs are commonly and collectively referred to as cur dogs. They are the Blue Lacy or Texas Blue Lacy, Catahoula Cur Dog, Kemmer Cur Dog, Leopard Cur Dog, Mountain Cur Dog, Southern Black Mouth Cur Dog, and Yellow Black Mouth Cur Dog.

Curs weigh around forty-five to forty-nine pounds. They are from twenty to twenty-six inches in height and have short, smooth coats. A cur is an all-purpose dog, able to do several different jobs—herding, guarding, hunting, and family member. The original curs controlled sheep and cattle that were not today's meek and mild farm animals but ancestral stock that fought for survival from the predators that existed in Europe and Asia thousands of years ago. The cur was the rootstock of most of the herding dogs in Europe, the Americas, and Australia.

An American farm dog original, the English Shepherd is related to both the Border Collie and the Australian Shepherd.

Dutch Shepherd

Just as there are four varieties of Belgian Shepherd, there are three varieties of Dutch Shepherd, distinguished by coat type. In the Netherlands, the breeds are called Langhaar Hollandse (long coat), Ruwhaar Hollandse (wire coat), and Korthaar Hollandse (short coat). Like their Belgian cousins, the Dutch Shepherds are multitalented herding dogs that are used as farm dogs as well as military, police, and service dogs.

Dutch Shepherds range from twenty-two to twenty-five inches in height and weigh between sixty-five and sixty-seven pounds. The Longhaired's coat is long, flat, straight, and harsh; the Shorthaired has a fine, dense coat; and the Wirehaircd's coat is rough to the touch and of medium length. All three coat types do well in cold climates. The Dutch Shepherd's coat is brindle-patterned in gray, yellow, silver, red, or gold and also comes in solid blue.

English Shepherd

Despite its name, the English Shepherd is truly an American breed. It is an all-around farm dog found throughout the Midwest and

Like the other Swiss mountain dogs, the Entlebucher, the smallest of the quartet, possesses the characteristic tricolor markings.

eastern United States. The English Shepherd is agile and quick, with the stamina and grit to cover many miles over all types of terrain. It has keen senses and can trail lost or injured animals. Calm in disposition, the English Shepherd will withstand the pressure of long hours of demanding work.

English Shepherds stand eighteen to twenty-three inches in height. Males weigh from forty-five to sixty pounds; females, forty to fifty pounds. They resemble the Australian Shepherd, with a medium-length coat.

Entlebucher (Entlebucher Mountain Dog and Entlebucher Cattle Dog)

The Entlebucher is the smallest member of Switzerland's Sennenhunds, the country's Mountain Dog family that also includes the Appenzeller, Bernese Mountain Dog, and Greater Swiss Mountain Dog. The Entlebucher's temperament is full of contradiction. It is devoted and loyal yet headstrong. It is smart and serious at work but playful at other times. On the whole, it has a friendly, pleasant personality and enjoys being around people and other dogs. These beautiful dogs are wonderful pets that are easily trained. They also become very attached to their owners.

Entlebuchers range from seventeen to twenty inches in height and weigh from forty-seven to sixty-two pounds. They are exceptionally clean and require little grooming. Their coat is short, thick, hard, and glossy. It is tricolored black, white, and rust, with the rust always between the black and white. There are also symmetrical markings on the toes, chest, and blaze. The Greater Swiss Mountain Dog's dense coat is approximately one and one-quarter inch to two inches long, compared with the Bernese Mountain Dog's somewhat longer coat.

Finnish Lapphund

Weatherproof Finnish Lapphunds are still used for herding reindeer in Finland. By nature, they are stable, intelligent, willing, and affectionate. They are protective and make good family watchdogs. They are energetic, love to run, and do best in a home with a yard. When young, some Lapphunds have a tendency to nip at the heels or hands of their owners, but this behavior can easily be corrected.

The Finnish Lapphund is a medium-size spitz. Males range from eighteen and one-half to twenty-one inches in height; females, from sixteen to eighteen and one-half inches. The coat is plentiful. They have long dense hair with a long smooth outercoat similar to a Samoyed's.

The Finnish Lapphund's almond-shaped eyes distinguish it from its Swedish counterpart, the Swedish Lapphund.

The German Shepherd Dog began its career as a herding dog only to become the world's most accomplished working dog.

German Shepherd Dog

The familiar German Shepherd is a large, strong, handsome dog. This is a direct, fearless, eager, and alert breed. It is known for its intelligence and great learning ability. The German Shepherd excels in many activities including Schutzhund, tracking, obedience, agility, and flyball.

German Shepherds weigh from seventy-seven to eighty-five pounds. The males range from twenty-four to twenty-six inches in height; the females, twenty-two to twenty-four inches. They sport a dense, double coat of medium length, neither short nor long. They vary in color and are heavy, constant shedders.

Hangin' Tree Cowdog

Developed by Gary Ericsson and named for his breeding prefix, the Hangin' Tree Cowdog is known for its courage and tenacity and its superior ability to handle any kind of cattle. It is the product of the careful breeding of four different dogs. From the Catahoula Leopard Dog it gets top hunting instincts, tenacity, and a natural trailing ability. From the Border Collie come intelligence, trainability, and gathering and herding skills. From the Australian Kelpie it gains agility, hardiness, and endurance. The Australian Shepherd Black Bear contributed his tough cattle skills.

It is a medium-size dog bred specifically for working cattle. Its short, straight, easily maintained outercoat protects it from heat and sheds burs well.

Icelandic Sheepdog

The Icelandic Sheepdog, Iceland's only native dog, is also known as the Icelandic Spitz or Iceland Dog. This breed is gentle, intelligent, and generally good-natured. At one time it was dangerously near extinction; although its popularity has increased, its numbers are still very small. Icelandic Sheepdogs are tough and energetic dogs, having evolved over many centuries in the harsh Icelandic climate. They are useful for herding and driving livestock in pastures and in the mountains.

They range in height from twelve to sixteen inches and weigh about twenty to thirty pounds. with prick ears and a curled tail. There are two coat types, long and short; both are extremely weatherproof. Both have double coats; the topcoat is fairly coarse, and the undercoat is thick and soft.

Lancashire Heeler

Little is known about the origin of this breed. Most sources say that the Lancashire Heeler is a cross between the Manchester Terrier and the Welsh Corgi. Heelers are small, powerful, sturdily built, alert, energetic workers. Built low to the ground, they have short legs in proportion to the rest of their body. Their ears are erect. Capable of herding cattle, goats, and horses, these little dogs have such a strong herding instinct that they must be taught not to nip at people's heels. They are difficult to obedience train.

One of the world's classic Nordic sheepdogs, the Icelandic Sheepdog is Iceland's only purebred dog breed.

The black-and-tan herder known as the Lancashire Heeler performs work similar to that of the Welsh Corgis.

Hardly your average farm dog, the Lapponian Herder was developed in Finland to drive reindeer.

The adult Heeler reaches ten to twelve inches in height and weighs six to thirteen pounds. Easy to groom, the Heeler's coat is plush, sleek, and shiny.

Lapponian Herder (Lapinporokoira and Lapland Reindeer Dog)

Lapponian Herders are described by the Lapphund Club of Finland as a genuine Finnish herding spitz. They are faithful family companion dogs with natural herding and territorial instincts. Hardy, muscular, and medium-size, Lapponian Herders have friendly dispositions and learn quickly. With its weatherproof coat, the breed is well adapted to life outdoors, but it can live indoors as long as it gets outdoor play and exercise. Lapponian Herders weigh up to sixty-six pounds and are nineteen to twenty-two inches in height. The breed's black or black and tan coat is medium-short, stiff, and coarse with a dense undercoat.

McNab (McNab Border Collie and McNab Sheepdog)

Dating back to the 1870s or earlier, these dogs began as Scotch Collies bred by the McNab family on their ranch in Mendocino, California. McNabs are well-mannered dogs, obedient, hardworking, and water-loving. These dogs have been bred primarily for performance in working stock. The McNab originated in the United States and is registered with the National Stock Dog Registry, but it is not recognized by any major kennel club.

It is medium to large in size, alert, and cat-footed. McNabs vary widely in weight, from as little as forty pounds to as much as seventy pounds. Their coat is black with white markings. The tail is not bushy; some McNabs have natural bobtails, and others have long, narrow, short-furred tails.

Mudi

In 1930, the Mudi was separated from the Puli and Pumi as a distinct breed. Previously, these three types of Hungarian herding dog were classified together. Today the Mudi, rare even in its native Hungary, is a tough, versatile farm dog. It herds cattle, guards its owners and their property, kills rats, and is sometimes used in groups of two or more for hunting boars (by circling the prey and trapping it in place until the hunter comes and makes the kill). It is intelligent, capable of making independent decisions and adapting to different situations and environments. It is also loyal, quick to react when provoked, and ready to defend and to fight.

The Mudi ranges from fourteen to twenty inches in height and weighs on average eighteen to twenty-nine pounds, although adults can weigh as much as thirty-five pounds. It is easy to groom—occasional combing and brushing of its dense, wavy coat is all that is needed—and sheds once or twice a year.

The versatile Mudi is four dogs in one: herder, hunter, guard, and terrier.

Devised to work on the *bu* (farm), the Norwegian Buhund is a compact, bright, and affectionate spitz breed.

New Zealand Huntaway

New Zealand Huntaways come in a wide variety of shapes, sizes, colors, and coat types. To New Zealand Huntaway fanciers, the dog's appearance or conformation is not as important as its working ability, but the breed generally weighs fifty-five to eighty pounds and stands about twenty to twenty-four inches tall. It is a highly intelligent breed and very much a one-man dog. It is the product of crossing many different breeds, with genetic contributions from the black Labrador Retriever, Hound, Border Collie, and German Shepherd Dog, among others. The New Zealand Huntaway is a breed that urges sheep forward by barking. Although it is not currently recognized by any kennel club registry, this breed is becoming increasingly popular as a companion dog.

Norwegian Buhund (Norwegian Sheepdog, Norwegian Farm Dog)

Like most other Nordic dogs, the Norwegian Buhunds (translated as stock or farm dogs) are clean, intelligent, and fun. They have a great deal of energy and desire for human companionship. They are very affectionate, love giving kisses, and are known for their fondness for children. They need a firm, consistent master, as they are headstrong, but they learn quickly.

The males range from seventeen to eighteen and one-half inches in height; females, from sixteen to seventeen and one-half inches. Males weigh from thirty-one to forty pounds; females, from twenty-six to thirty-five pounds. The outercoat is smooth and harsh, while the undercoat is soft and woolly. They should be brushed regularly and are seasonal heavy shedders.

Old English Sheepdog (Bobtail)

The Old English Sheepdog is a very adaptable breed. It is friendly, intelligent, and gentle; likes to stick close to home; and has a well-deserved reputation as a great family companion. Old English Sheepdogs are known for their affectionate, endearing personalities and their ability to steal your heart. They are competent herding dogs but at times stubbornly do things their own way.

Males range from twenty-two to twenty-four inches in height; females, from twenty to twenty-two inches. Adult males weigh roughly sixty-five pounds; females, up to sixty pounds.

The Old English Sheepdog's coat is famously profuse. Its texture is described as hard, not straight, but shaggy and free from curl. The undercoat is a waterproof pile. It requires constant upkeep: unless it is brushed at least three times a week, it becomes matted and leads to skin problems. It also sheds seasonally, usually during the spring.

Old German Shepherd (Altdeutsche Schäferhunde)

The forerunner of the modern German Shepherd Dog is still living in Germany today. In fact, 90% of the canine work on the sheep flocks of Germany is still performed by this nonstandard precursor of our standard German Shepherd. In 1990, an association called the AAA (Arbeitsgemeinschaft zur Zucht Altdeutscher Hütehunde) was created to

With more coat than the sheep it herds, the shaggy Old English Sheepdog is an unusual choice for a working dog, although the breed excels as a companion and show dog.

preserve and protect this venerable breed. The several types of the Old German Shepherd are on the larger, heavier end of the medium-size herding breeds.

Ovelheiro Gaúcho

The Ovelheiro Gaúcho originated in Brazil as a sheepdog, but it has developed into an excellent cowdog as well. The Portuguese name means "Gaucho Shepherd," given to the breed by Brazilian cowboys known as gauchos. This breed is officially recognized only in Brazil, where it is still used to herd both sheep and cattle. It possesses both the top qualities of a shepherd and the more forceful nature demanded of a cattle dog. The breed is also used to protect its herd or flock from predators and human trespassers. The Ovelheiro Gaúcho is intelligent and learns commands easily. The breed is also said to be adaptable and willing to please.

It is a medium-size dog: both males and females range from twenty-one and one-half to twenty-five and one-half inches in height.

The ancient Picardy Shepherd requires a confident and devoted owner in order to thrive in any environment.

Picardy Shepherd (Berger Picard)

The Picardy Shepherd is a rare herding dog that hails from France. It is possibly the oldest of all the French shepherding breeds. The temperament of this breed may be uneven: a Picardy Shepherd may be at times reserved, suspicious, inquisitive, vivacious, or tranquil. These dogs need to be well socialized. They should not be isolated in a kennel, and they need daily reassuring attention from their owners.

Physically, this breed is well muscled and slightly longer than it is tall. An adult weighs from fifty to seventy pounds and stands from twenty-one to twenty-five inches at the shoulder. Its waterproof coat is harsh to the touch; it needs to be brushed only once or twice a month. The Picardy Shepherd is a very light shedder and has no doggy odor.

Polish Lowland Sheepdog (Polski Owczarek Nizinny)

The bobtailed, cobby, medium-size shaggy Polish Lowland Sheepdog is stable and self-confident. It needs a dominant master and consistent training from a very young age. This breed is loyal, somewhat aloof, and slightly suspicious of strangers. It is strong and muscular.

Males range from eighteen to twenty inches in height; females, seventeen to nineteen inches. The long, thick, and shaggy double coat is nearly straight or slightly wavy. The undercoat is soft and dense. Typically, hanging hair covers the eyes.

The Polish Lowland Sheepdog is sometimes called a PON, an acronym for its Polish name, Polski Owczarek Nizinny.

Puli

The Puli is an ancient breed of Hungarian sheepdog. It is sturdy and durable, a superb athlete with quick reflexes that allow it to turn on a dime and clear a six-foot fence from a standstill. These are playful dogs that make excellent companions. They are self-confident and bounce with energy and insatiable curiosity.

The Hungarian Puli adorns itself in rough cords that protect the dog from weather and possible adversaries.

The Puli sheds less than many other breeds. Its coat clumps together easily, and if allowed to develop naturally will form tassel-like cords. The coat is the result of a controlled matting process and needs considerable attention to stay neat, clean, and attractive. The woolly cords vary in shape and thickness, either flat or round depending on the texture of the coat and the balance of undercoat to outercoat.

The males are seventeen inches and females are sixteen inches from the withers to the ground, with an acceptable range of an inch over or under these measurements. Females can weigh twenty-three to twenty-five pounds, males slightly more. The Puli is a solid-colored dog that can be black, white, gray, or a cream color, the latter with or without a black mask.

Pumi

The Pumi is not as well known as its fellow Hungarian sheepdog, the Puli. Its most notable physical characteristic is its hairy, upright, folded-tip ears, which are constantly moving since nothing

Ever alert, as its unique ears convey, the Pumi fulfills the role of farm dog with style and devotion.

escapes this dog's attention. It is easily taught and interested in everything that's going on. Pumis are very affectionate but usually bond to just one person in a family. They have the temperament of the traditional working dog they were bred to be, with strong herding instincts. Their working behaviors (chasing, nipping, poking, and barking) may be inappropriate in a normal household setting.

Adult Pumis are thirteen to nineteen inches in height and weigh from eighteen to thirty-three pounds. They are easy to groom: the braided medium-length coat does not mat easily, and an occasional brushing is all that is needed.

Pyrenean Shepherd (Berger des Pyrenees, Petite Berger, Labrit)

The Pyrenean Shepherd is the oldest and smallest of the French herding dogs. It is a lively dog with quick reflexes; in World War I, the Berger des Pyrenees was used on the battlefield to carry messages and search for the wounded. It is long and lean, fifteen to nineteen inches and fifteen to thirty-two pounds.

Few shepherds employ Samoyeds today, although their natural beauty and pearly whites have made up for the lack of job opportunities to herd reindeer.

Known as the shaggy shepherd, this breed has a medium to long shaggy, coarse, water-resistant coat. There are two varieties: one has hair all over its body and the other has shorter hair on the face (smooth muzzled, or *face-rase*). Fawn is the most prevalent color, but it also appears in black or blue merle. Moderate grooming is required.

Samoyed

Traditionally a herder, though more of a working and companion dog today, the breed takes its name from the Samoyedic peoples of Siberia. An alternative name, especially in Europe, is Bjelkier. Nomadic reindeer herders bred the white, smiling dogs to help with the herding, pull sleds, and, in this frozen region, keep their owners warm at night by sleeping with them.

Although highly intelligent, the Samoyed can be difficult to train, for it has a mind of its own. It quickly tires of repetitive training and responds better to motivation than to correction. Samoyeds' friendly disposition makes them poor guard dogs but excellent companions, especially for small children or even other dogs, and they remain playful into old age. Their herding instinct is strong, and they will often attempt to turn and redirect their human companions, especially when playing with children. The breed is characterized by an alert and happy expression.

Males typically weigh forty-four to sixty pounds; females, thirty-seven to fifty-five pounds. They require considerable grooming to prevent matting, as they shed profusely, leaving hair everywhere, sometimes once but usually twice a year. Grooming is also important to a Samoyed's comfort during hot, humid summer months. Samoyeds have a dense double-layer coat. The top layer contains long, coarse, straight guard hairs that protect the soft, dense, woolly, all-season undercoat, which appears white but has a hint of silver coloring. This weatherproof top layer keeps the undercoat relatively clean and free of debris. Dirt typically falls from the outer layer of fur with little work, so despite its length and thickness the coat is easy to keep very clean-looking.

More than just a shaggy pretty face, the Schapendoes is a hardy working dog who's energetic, protective, and reliable.

Schapendoes (Dutch Sheepdog)

The Schapendoes is a shaggy dog from Holland recognizable by its long dense coat, usually blue-gray to black mixed with white. It is a well-

Among the most popular herding dogs in the world, the Shetland Sheepdog resembles the Rough Collie in miniature.

proportioned, well-muscled dog with an intelligent expression and lively temperament. The breed is affectionate, obedient, tractable, alert, faithful, and reliable. Schapendoes have been in existence for hundreds of years; however, they are not very well known. The breed is physically similar to the Beardie, Nizinny, and Puli and is likely descended from the same basic stock as the Briard and Bergamasco. Schapendoes weigh about thirty-three pounds and stand from sixteen to twenty inches.

Shetland Sheepdog

Shetland Sheepdogs, or Shelties as they are often called, resemble a Collie in miniature, but Shelties are not miniature or toy Collies. The Sheltie is a distinct breed and was not bred down from the Collie. The breed originated on the Shetland Islands, off the northeast coast of Scotland. Over the years, the breed was developed as an all-purpose farm dog, guard dog, and affectionate and loyal companion.

Shetland Sheepdogs stand between thirteen and sixteen inches at the shoulder. They come in colors of black, blue merle, and sable (ranging from golden through mahogany), marked with varying amounts of white and/or tan. They are double coated. The outercoat is long, straight, and harsh; the undercoat is short, furry, and extremely dense.

Shiloh Shepherd

The Shiloh Shepherd is powerfully built, with unsurpassed beauty and elegance. A breed still under development, the Shiloh is similar to the German Shepherd Dog except bigger. With rare smaller exceptions, males average thirty to thirty-one inches in height and weigh 115–135 pounds. Females average twenty-eight to twenty-nine inches in height (although today many reach thirty inches) and weigh 95–110 pounds. Extremely versatile and easy to train, Shiloh Shepherds are alert and happy dogs willing to work.

The Shiloh Shepherd is a recently developed herding and guarding breed, considered by its founders to be an improvement on the German Shepherd Dog.

The Shiloh's coat comes in two varieties: plush and smooth. The plush coat is medium to long with a dense undercoat and requires regular brushing. The smooth coat is thick and medium in length with a harsh outercoat that requires only minimal grooming. Both are seasonally heavy shedders. Shilohs should be bathed only a few times each year so as not to deplete the skin oils.

Standard Schnauzer (Mittelschnauzer, Schnauzer)

The oldest of the three schnauzer breeds (Standard, Giant, and Miniature), the Standard Schnauzer originated in southern Germany, where it was bred as a general farm dog and rat catcher. The first Standard Schnauzers were brought into the United States around 1900. This is a handsome, robust, squarely built, medium-size dog with a hard wiry coat in salt-and-pepper or solid black.

The Standard Schnauzer is active, energetic, and playful, with plenty of spirit and enthusiasm for a variety of work scenarios. The breed has been used reliably as police dogs, exterminators, and service dogs as well as herders. Highly intelligent and responsive, Schnauzers are eager to please, which makes training easy, and their territorial nature makes them effective watchdogs for families and livestock. The Standard Schnauzer gets along well with household pets with early socialization but can be aggressive with dogs of the same sex. The Standard Schnauzer's double coat requires considerable maintenance.

Males stand between eighteen and twenty inches high at the shoulders and weigh about forty to forty-five pounds; females range from seventeen to nineteen inches in height and weigh thirty-five to forty pounds.

The Standard Schnauzer is the oldest and most versatile of the three Schnauzer breeds developed in Germany.

Stumpy-Tail Cattle Dog

Although they share much the same history and appearance, the Stumpy-Tail Cattle Dog of Australia is a distinct breed from the Australian Cattle Dog. The Stumpy-Tail Cattle Dog is a cross of the old Smithfield, a black-and-white tailless herding dog, and the ubiquitous native Dingo. It is born with a tiny stumpy tail, which when fully grown measures no longer than four inches in length. Australian Stumpy-Tail Cattle Dogs are silent workers whose endurance is second to none. They are loyal and courageous. They weigh between thirty-five and forty-five pounds and are from seventeen to twenty inches in height. Their coat is medium-short, straight, harsh, and dense.

The Swedish Lapphund is as elegant as it is talented, serving as both herder and companion in its native land.

Not to be discounted as the gray version of the Welsh Corgis, the Swedish Vallhund offers more natural herding instinct and no less charm.

Swedish Lapphund (Lapland Spitz and Lapplandska Spets)

Swedish Lapphunds are the Swedish version of the Finnish herding spitz breed originally used for herding reindeer. Natural herders, they are still used for sheepherding in their native country, but today they are mainly companion and show dogs. Their affectionate and protective nature makes them good house pets and natural alarm dogs.

The Swedish Lapphund is a moderate-size breed: females are from sixteen to eighteen inches in height; males, eighteen to twenty inches. They range from forty-two to forty-six pounds. They have a substantial and weatherproof coat with a thick and woolly topcoat.

Swedish Vallhund (Vasgotaspets and Swedish Cattle Dog)

This is a robust breed with a strong, fairly long body. At first glance, the Vallhund resembles the Corgi. On closer inspection, however, it is clear that the Vallund has a longer leg and smaller, mobile ears. Its head is wedge-shaped, not foxy like the Corgi's head.

Swedish Vallhunds are intelligent, eager to please, and easy to train. This is a friendly, active breed with a typically vivacious spitz personality. Vallhunds are devoted to their owners; they are even-tempered and get along very well with children, protecting them from strangers. They love attention; although they can be a bit show-offish, their many abilities and spontaneous sense of humor make them a fine family companion.

Males range from thirteen to fourteen inches in height; females, from twelve to thirteen inches. Their coat is short and smooth and sheds just a little. The grooming requirements are not burdensome; a regular combing and brushing will keep the coat in good condition.

Texas Heelers

Texas Heelers are commonly a cross between a combination of Australian Cattle Dogs, Border Collies, and/or Australian Shepherds, bred strictly for their ability to boss cows.

Welsh Corgi (Cardigan and Pembroke)

Corgi in Welsh means "dwarf dog." Both types of Corgi are long and indeed short-legged and low to the ground. The more popular Pembroke Corgi, whose existence in Britain has been traced to at least AD 920, was originally used for livestock droving. Today both Pembrokes and Cardigans are still used for livestock droving but are more commonly kept as companion dogs. They became Kennel Club registered in 1928, were registered as separate breeds in the United Kingdom in 1934, and were

The Texas Heeler is the pride of the Lone Star State.

The more popular of the two Welsh dwarfs, the Pembroke Welsh Corgi flourishes in an active family and farm environment.

accepted by the American Kennel Club in 1936.

The Pembroke Corgi is an intelligent and active little dog. Ideally suited to the active family, it is obedient and loyal, good around children as long as it is treated with respect, and a capable watchdog. Females and males range from ten to twelve inches in height. Females weigh twenty-two to twenty-four pounds on average; males, twenty-two to twenty-six pounds.

The Cardigan Welsh Corgi is a small-size, sturdy little dog that is also set low to the ground. Although not as popular as its cousin, the Cardigan has a moderate temperament and makes an outstanding herding companion. It has a foxlike brush for a tail and a foxy head shape. It is much longer than it is tall. Females and males range in height from eleven to thirteen inches. Females can weigh anywhere from twenty-four to thirty-three pounds; males, from thirty-three to forty pounds.

The outercoats of Pembroke and Cardigan Corgis are medium-length, straight, and waterproof with a short, soft, thick undercoat. The outercoat is flat with outer guard hairs that are slightly harsh in texture but never wiry. Overall hair length varies, with slightly thicker and longer ruff around the neck, chest, and on the shoulders. The Corgi is a moderate shedder, and its coat needs regular brushing to remove loose and dead hairs. If Corgis have been out in the mud, it is easier to remove the dirt after it has dried. Corgis come in colors of brindle, sable, red, black and tan, and blue merle.

Welsh Sheepdog

Welsh Sheepdogs have been in existence well over 800 years in their native Wales. They are courageous and highly adaptable working dogs. They are intelligent, active, and alert, making them good guard dogs and watchdogs. They bark at intruders but are normally gentle and good with children. Their natural instincts for stock work and their ability to use their own initiative as well as follow their master's commands make them suitable for a variety of working situations.

The traditional sheepdogs of Wales were in danger of becoming extinct, so in 1997 the Welsh Sheepdog Society (WSS) was formed to preserve indigenous Welsh Sheepdogs and the role of the breed in livestock farming. The WSS describes the breed's working style: "They bark if needed, and will run across the backs of sheep if they become jammed. A strong dog can catch and hold a hill ewe at command. Most will catch a lamb for treatment."

The Welsh Sheepdog is a medium-size, well-proportioned breed that exhibits tremendous agility and stamina. It can be medium- or smooth-coated and comes in a variety of colors including black, black and tan, red, blue merle, or roan, with or without white markings.

Distinguished mainly by its fox-brush tail, the Cardigan Welsh Corgi is an adaptable, fast-working herder who is at once loyal and affectionate.

Herding dogs prove to be challenging companion animals, although the rewards far outweigh the difficulties their energy and intelligence present.

Chapter 3

Owning a Herding Dog

What are herding breeds like as pets? As a general rule, with some exceptions, herding breeds are not easy pets. Most are "workaholics," bred for endurance and performance over centuries. This is the nature of herding dogs, which are happiest when they have a job to do, whether that job is herding, obedience, agility, or any of the other active occupations and dog sports they excel at. Before you consider purchasing a herding dog, ask yourself whether your lifestyle and time schedule fit a herding dog's needs.

When selecting a herding dog, consider whether the breed's natural instincts are a good match for your family. Pictured is the author's nephew and friends.

Hanging out in an apartment or inside the house is too restrictive for most herding breeds. Likewise, confining a herding dog in a fenced outdoor area rarely works as an adequate place for exercise. Herding dogs need to be physically and mentally challenged. Typical pet owners often find herding breeds' high energy level too intense and demanding. These dogs can be hyperactive and destructive and possibly become a nuisance if not given something to do, so if you are unable to provide the exercise they require, you would be well advised to find a less active breed. Too often, dogs purchased for the wrong reasons are given away; dog ownership should be a long-term commitment, so choose realistically.

Herding dogs are intelligent and tend to learn quickly. This may seem like a good thing, but it can sometimes pose a problem. Herding dogs might learn things the owner didn't intend for them to learn, and some of these newly learned behaviors can be difficult to undo. Their high intelligence is one of the reasons they get bored and into trouble so easily. But then, it's also one of the reasons they excel in obedience, herding, agility, and many other dog sports.

Choosing a Breed

There are many factors to consider when choosing the right dog, and there are many herding breeds to choose from. Consider first whether herding dogs' natural instincts are a good match for your individual family members. For example, though many herding breeds are gentle with children, one of the most common reasons people give for surrendering a dog to a rescue shelter is that the dog nips or snaps at the children in the family. This is often not a sign of viciousness but rather a problem caused by their intense herding instinct. A few herding dogs treat children as if they are livestock. When a herding dog wants a child to do something and the child doesn't cooperate, the dog's instinct tells it to push harder, and they often nip quite hard. This instinct cannot be eliminated, but it can and must be controlled by consistent training. The most satisfied herding dog owners are people who enjoy spending a lot of time with their dogs and are willing to make the commitment to exercise and train that dog.

Most herding breeds have certain traits in common. Although each breed is best adapted to a particular climate, terrain, and stock-handling purpose, herding breeds can be described generally as intelligent working dogs with strong herding and guardian instincts. They are exceptional companions. Most are versatile and easily trained; most

Owners must consider carefully the characteristics of the breed they fancy. A lovable ball of energy can grow into an unruly, unreliable adult dog without proper rearing.

Many herding breeds are handsome dogs with beautiful distinctive coat colors.

perform assigned tasks with great ease, style, and enthusiasm. Most tend to be reserved around strangers but do not exhibit shyness. They are authoritative but not vicious, and are extremely active. Most are good-natured with even dispositions. Herding breeds tend to be deeply loyal, loving, and responsive to their owners. Despite their wariness around strangers, most can be trusted with considerate children.

Many herding breeds are handsome dogs with beautiful or distinctive coats. All coats of pure breeds should be rich and clear. Colors described as blue merle are silver-flecked with dark, deep gray and patches of black. Red merles have flecks of rich liver, deep sorrel, or cinnamon-and-sugar throughout the coat. They also come in solid black and solid red. All can have white markings and/or tan (copper) points, with no order of preference. Most breeds of herding dogs have coats that are weather-resistant.

Choosing a breed, however, should never be based solely on its appearance. Compare breeds' size, temperament, and activity level before you purchase any dog. Not all herding breeds are alike, so learn as much as you can about many different herding breeds before selecting the breed that is right for you.

For example, breeds like the Australian Cattle Dog and Briard, although exceptional companions in many ways, can be somewhat hard-headed. These breeds at times do not work well for more than one trainer. And some Collies, for instance, may not have the intensity desired for hard work on a cattle ranch. These differences do not mean one breed is superior to another. They are, however, good to know as you decide what traits you want in your dog.

There are several ways to get useful information about the different breeds' temperaments and specific requirements. Books and Web sites can be helpful starting points, but there is no substitute for attending herding trials, dog shows, and training clinics where you can observe a variety of herding breeds in action, in person, and learn the characteristics that define the breed standards.

A breed standard describes the physical and temperamental characteristics that enable the breed to perform at its highest level. A breed standard, a written description of "type," is also a model toward which all breeders strive. It is the standard of excellence and also the blueprint that show judges use to evaluate entries in the ring. A breed standard will include the general appearance, character/temperament, head, teeth, eyes, ears, neck, topline, body, forequarters, hindquarters, coat, color, gait, size, proportion, substance, and sometimes disqualifications of the breed. Complete breed standards can be obtained through the American Kennel Club, the United Kennel Club, or a specific breed club, such as the

The allure of a well-bred Collie puppy is quite ineffable; breeders call this quality "type."

A Bouvier des Flandres puppy in the less commonly seen fawn coloration.

Australian Shepherd Club of America or the American Border Collie Association.

There is no one perfect herding breed. That's why you must find the one breed that is best suited to your individual needs and desires. Ask yourself these practical questions when considering getting a herding dog: What am I looking for in a dog? What environment am I bringing a dog into? How much food does the dog eat and can I afford it? How much time will the dog need from me and do I have that much time to spare? Will I train the dog? If not, who will?

Naturally, if you are planning to work a herding dog, you need to consider the type of stock work you expect it to do. As far as working styles, herding breeds can be divided into close-running loose-eyed breeds—meaning the dog tends to nip and bark at the edge of the herd without making constant eye contact—and the wider-running medium-eyed and strong-eyed dogs, which tend to work in a crouching posture and can intimidate stock animals with their stare. They can be further divided between cowdogs and sheepdogs. Breeds developed to handle hogs or cattle are apt to be more assertive on livestock and may not be as suitable for working sheep.

Practical considerations for a companion herding dog include its size compared with the accommodations you can provide, its personality type, and its grooming requirements. Find out how much a particular breed sheds, for example. Most herding breeds shed some, and even the ones that don't still need to be trimmed. Seasonal shedding is normal; light year-round shedding is normal in dogs kept indoors under artificial light. Some breeds require intensive grooming several times a week, while others require very little. Case in point: Old English Sheepdogs must be brushed often to prevent mats, and their feet and rear need to be trimmed for cleanliness. If stray hairs on your navy blue suit or dog hair on your light-colored carpet bothers you, chances are you will be frustrated by owning a herding dog through no fault of its own.

Choosing a Breeder

Choosing the right puppy or dog begins with finding an experienced, reputable breeder. Anyone can put two dogs together, let them mate, and call himself a "breeder." However, being a reputable breeder encompasses far more than that. Reputable breeders offer only sound dogs with desirable temperaments for sale. You won't find a reputable breeder trying to sell dogs to local pet stores or advertising in newspaper classified sections. Good breeders do not need sales gimmicks and do not deal with unqualified or unscreened buyers. They rely on the quality of their dogs and on recommendations from satisfied customers. They also advertise in breed club publications.

It's never a good idea to purchase a dog from a newspaper or any other source that advertises a dog as "rare." Rare can sometimes mean that the dog has faults or show-ring disqualifications (such as "a rare blue Corgi" or "a rare solid white Australian Shepherd"). Most people who do not know better might purchase a dog advertised as rare and later find out the dog is deaf or has serious health issues. Steer clear of this sales gimmick.

When you meet the breeder face-to-face, you will be able to judge for yourself how well she cared for the litter.

Before purchasing a puppy, check out several breeders' facilities. Make sure their dogs are kept in a clean and healthy environment. Ask to see where the dogs are kept and to meet the sire (if on the premises) and dam of the litter. If the breeder insists on bringing only the pups to you, be somewhat cautious.

Dog breeding should be pursued with a sense of pride and for a sense of fulfillment more than financial

Responsible breeders never release puppies until they are fully weaned and ready to go to new homes, usually between eight and ten weeks of age.

You may be able to adopt an older puppy from a breeder who has held on to puppies to gauge their show quality or working promise.

gain. Once you find a breeder you think you want to deal with, it is a good idea to check references. If the breeder is unable to provide references, you should perhaps move on. Talk to other breeders, rescue groups, veterinarians, or anyone else who can give you information about the breeder you plan to purchase your dog from.

Good breeders care about the quality of their litters. They control breeding to insure that the high standards of the breed are maintained after a puppy's sale. For example, many breeders require buyers to sign a limited registration contract, especially in connection with purebred show-quality dogs. This type of contract means you are legally obligated to not breed your dog. If you are purchasing a dog with hopes of someday breeding it, consider this important restriction. Many breeders require buyers to sign a spay/neuter contract for dogs that are pet quality. A dog deemed as pet quality lacks the excellence in conformation that is expected of dogs intended for the show ring. Your promise to spay or neuter your pup assures the breeder that breed quality will not be further diluted (and that the pet population will stay under control).

Breeders will be familiar with the bloodlines of their dogs for several generations. The bloodline should be one that is tested and used for herding. Puppies themselves must be structurally sound and free from any genetic diseases that would interfere with herding. Keep in mind when looking for a dog to work livestock that the litter should be from working ancestors who have proved to be mentally and physically sound.

Exceptional breeders encourage you to select a puppy with the temperament and personality that are compatible with you and your family. Do not let the breeder convince you that "this" one is for you. The breeder should be knowledgeable about each puppy's characteristics and honestly describe both good points and bad points.

Find out if your breeder is involved in breed-related activities. You will find that most good breeders participate in a wide variety of activities including showing, herding trials and tests, agility, flyball, or involvement in local club or rescue groups. A concerned breeder cares about the future of the breed and his dogs. In dealing with a good breeder you will be assured that you are getting what you pay for.

As you can see, choosing a reputable breeder involves more than finding a phone number in the newspaper. Be sure to educate yourself before making a decision to purchase. Before meeting with a prospective breeder, write down some questions, know the breed, and be patient. Choosing the right breeder and pup is not something that you should rush into.

Breeders who are highly regarded try to improve the breed and produce the best puppies possible. They breed dogs that closely match the breed standard. They will provide you with a written contract and health guarantee, or at least an oral agreement, with clear terms that you can live with. A health guarantee certifies that the dog is structurally sound and free from heritable diseases that could interfere with his ability to work. Good breeders will also provide you with registration papers, the pedigree, and up-to-date shot and health records.

Most important, choose a breeder who is willing to mentor you as necessary through the dog's life. Good breeders will provide you with follow-up advice and answer questions to help you get off to a good start with your new puppy. Remember, you are purchasing a dog that will be with you for twelve to fifteen years. That is why it's important to choose the right breeder and the right dog.

Selecting the Perfect Puppy

To select the puppy that is just right for you, be prepared to conduct a number of temperament tests yourself at the breeder's facility. Most of these tests are based on the research of William Campbell, a well-known canine behaviorist.

The evaluation should be conducted in an area (a room or fenced yard) that is unfamiliar to the puppy, with as few distractions as possible. The puppies you will be considering should be awake and active for at least ten to fifteen minutes before you begin the evaluation, which should take place well before or sufficiently after feeding time.

Give yourself enough time to evaluate each puppy in the litter individually. Handle each gently without verbally praising or urging him on during the evaluation. The goal is to choose a puppy that is outgoing, friendly, attentive, and willing to attempt whatever you want him to do. Ideally, he will show you that he has a good-natured, adaptable character, provided he is trained and handled correctly.

If a gentle nature suits you best, rule out the more dominant, aggressive breeds. Look for a herding dog prospect that is slightly submissive and less self-confident; that readily looks to you for leadership; and that is affectionate, gentle, and easy to handle.

Social Attraction

The first evaluation tests how readily the puppy comes when called. It also reveals innate confidence, curiosity, anxiety, or fearfulness.

In this assessment, immediately on entering the test area, the puppy is placed on the ground or on the floor of the room; the tester stands aside, ignoring him. The puppy is allowed to explore the area for a few seconds. Then the tester kneels down, gently claps hands, and calls the puppy with happy, repetitive tones, "Here puppy, puppy." The puppy should react quickly, stop whatever he is doing, and immediately and willingly go to the tester. He should allow himself to be

Born to herd—this litter of Border Collie puppies is making the acquaintance of a future woolly charge.

petted without biting, growling, or showing other signs of aggression.

A puppy is not necessarily less desirable if he must be called more than once before responding, as long as he then stays with the tester. It is, however, less desirable if the puppy must be called a second time and then stays with the tester only briefly. A puppy that is indifferent, inattentive, fearful, or aggressive is displaying undesirable traits.

Following

The second test should start with the tester in position next to the puppy. The tester should walk away from the puppy in a normal manner. The tester should observe the pup closely while walking to make sure the puppy actually sees the tester walk away; otherwise, mere lack of awareness might be incorrectly interpreted as independence. The most desirable result is for the puppy to

In testing the puppy's temperament, alertness and responsiveness should shine through. Look at the keen expression on this puppy's face.

readily follow the tester. Puppies that get under foot, nip at testers' heels (exhibiting dominant traits), or follow reluctantly or not at all may be too difficult to train for the average person.

Restraint

In the third test, the puppy should be picked up slowly with both the tester's arms slightly outstretched. One hand supports the body while the other hand supports the puppy's neck. The puppy should be gently placed on his back for thirty seconds. How readily the puppy accepts this position or how fiercely it objects to this position is an indication of how trusting and compliant or dominant is its nature, respectively. Most puppies will struggle, but an ideal puppy will settle and make eye contact or, still acceptably, struggle but settle. Puppies that struggle fiercely, thrash about, growl, or attempt to bite are not the best choices as a herding prospect for the average person to train; neither are puppies that show no struggle and avoid eye contact.

Retrieving

The fourth test reveals willingness, intelligence, trust, and hunting instincts. Retrieving is closely correlated with willingness to work, self-confidence, and intelligence.

Roll a ball past the puppy's nose so he can easily follow the object. Preferably, the puppy chases the ball without hesitation; picks up the ball; and then plays with it, carries it around, or brings it back to the tester. Note that success in this test does not depend on the puppy's returning the ball to the tester.

In this evaluation, it is less desirable for the puppy to pay more attention to the tester and only hesitantly follow the ball or toy. It

A puppy who is reluctant to follow a person may present difficulties further down the road, when basic obedience lessons commence.

Retrieving with enthusiasm demonstrates a puppy's willingness to work as well as his hunting instincts.

is undesirable for puppies to show no interest in the object. If the puppies are not fully awake, the evaluation will not produce accurate results. It is important that these tests be done only after the puppies have been awake for at least ten to fifteen minutes.

These exercises are useful indicators of a puppy's basic nature and trainability, but be sure to consider your gut feeling about a particular pup as well. Most of us know the right puppy when we see him.

The Responsible Owner

Many responsibilities come with owning a new puppy. Everyone knows how irresistible and precious puppies are. To make sure your puppy becomes a healthy adult dog, you must provide a healthy environment at all stages of his life. As puppies, they require daily care, much the same as a human baby would. Puppies need food, fresh water, shelter, clean dry bedding, house-training, and most of all lots of love and attention. You must be willing to clean up their waste, before and after they are house-trained. You must be willing to take the time to train, exercise, and play with your puppy. The decision to add a dog to your family, puppy or adult, should not be taken lightly.

As your puppy grows into an older dog, his basic needs remain the same. He will always need safe shelter, dry bedding, and protection from the elements. Dogs can suffer from too much heat or too much cold. Whether your dog lives inside your house or outside in a fenced yard, he should have his own special spot that is his alone.

All dogs need clean fresh water all the time. Keep a bowl of water where your dog can easily get to it. Some dogs love to play in their water bowls and tip them over or stand in them. In this case, you may have to check and refill his water

Once you've identified a litter of potentially excellent candidates, making the final selection will require the breeder's counsel and experience.

bowl twice a day. It is important for your dog to stay well hydrated.

Preparing for the Puppy

Preparing for a new pup is much the same as preparing for the arrival of a new baby. Before you bring your puppy home, make a list of the things he will need and put them in place. Basic canine care includes fiberglass crate or wire kennel, safe puppy toys such as a rubber ball and chewable or squeaky toys, a collar and leash,

Bringing a curious, full-of-beans herding puppy into your home requires preparation and patience, not to mention weewee pads.

puppy food, nonchewable and nonbreakable water and food bowls, a grooming brush, nail clippers, tearless baby shampoo, clean-up materials, and a basic first aid kit. If you will keep your pup indoors, also consider carpet and stain remover and a baby gate.

Remember to puppy-proof your home. If you have ever had a new puppy before, you will remember that nothing is safe. As puppies grow, they chew on everything. Watch out for and remove small objects that can be swallowed; common small items that require surgical removal if swallowed include small toys, jacks, marbles, pins, needles, pencils, and things that could splinter such as chicken bones, glass, or wood.

Make sure you keep potential poisons out of a puppy's reach. Antifreeze, many kinds of lawn and garden products, and other chemicals typically stored in the garage should be moved to a secure place to which even a determined puppy will not have access. (Refer to the section on signs of poisoning in chapter 7.)

Puppies need to chew when they teethe. This is a natural part of the growth process. They will chew on furniture legs, houseplants, throw rugs, and anything else on the floor. A puppy also will chew on almost anything that dangles within reach, such as toilet paper or electrical cords. Be sure to empty trash cans and put away your shoes when they are not on your feet. You get the idea. If you don't want something chewed up, remove it or keep the puppy away from it. Puppies do not like the smell of cloves, so a dab of clove oil on precious furniture may deter a teething puppy. Keep in mind that puppies also will chew on the hands and feet of humans of all ages, so closely supervise puppies around young children.

Arriving Home

When you arrive home with the new pup, allow him to explore his new world. It is important for him to discover and become comfortable with his new territory and the people around him. He will probably be frightened at first by the bombardment of unfamiliar sights, smells, and sounds, so let him run about freely through the house and yard, keeping an eye on him, steering him clear of off-limits areas, and responding to him calmly and reassuringly.

This Australian Cattle Dog urchin defines *rowdy* in the herding-dog world.

Set all myths aside: crate training is the best way to house-train a young puppy.

The best time to bring your puppy home is at the beginning of a weekend. This will give you time to acquaint your puppy with his new home and to begin housebreaking. Even at the age of eight weeks, your puppy is able and ready to begin learning where he may eat, drink, sleep, and go to the bathroom.

The first night away from his mom and his other littermates can be difficult for both you and your new puppy. Expect the puppy to cry and even bark a bit when you put him down for the night. Provide a clean, dry, comfortable place to sleep. I suggest putting your new bundle of wonder into a crate or kennel each night for sleeping. Sleeping in the crate will give your puppy a sense of security and ease his adjustment to life away from the litter. As your puppy gets used to the kennel, he will actually prefer sleeping there. I have found it helpful to place a ticking clock alongside the pup when he is put down for the night. The tick of the clock reminds him of the sound of his mother's heartbeat. Very soft music played at low volume may also soothe the puppy and help him relax and settle down. His crate will eventually become the pup's private den. When you are unable to keep an eye on him, the crate is a good place to keep him out of harm's way. It will become his safe haven.

Make sure the crate is large enough for him to stretch out in. It should be tall enough to allow him to stand comfortably with his head in a natural posture. Crates can be purchased at many retailers and come in many different sizes.

When you first introduce your new puppy to his crate, make it a pleasant experience. Place a couple of doggy treats inside the crate, and let the puppy go in to retrieve them. At first, keep the puppy in the crate for short periods, gradually lengthening the duration as he becomes accustomed to his crate. As the puppy grows, he will be comfortable in this crate for several hours at a time.

Remember that your puppy will need lots and lots of love, socialization, and exercise. A dog that receives all of these things will be a happy well-adjusted adult.

House-Training

Feed your puppy on a regular schedule, and house-training will be easy. Every time you feed or water him, take him outside a few minutes later and stay with him until he relieves himself. Every time your puppy wakes from a nap, take him outside. The first thing to do in the morning is let him out of his crate or kennel and immediately take him outside. The last thing to do before putting him in his crate at night is take him outside.

On every occasion, praise him once he has completed his business. Puppies do not have any more control than new babies do, but they learn. Most accidents can be traced to neglect or an inconsistent schedule. Understand your puppy's natural behaviors and apply them in training. In the wild, young pups learn at an early age to go far from their den to defecate. If the pup is confined to his crate, he has no other choice than to soil his bed unless you let him out when he needs to go.

If you follow consistent training practices from the start, your puppy

A good back-up plan to housebreaking a puppy is paper training, which might be useful in some living situations.

Cleaning Tips

These tips come in handy when dealing with cleaning up after accidents and controlling various odors caused by your dog.

- Neutralize the odor of urine on a carpet with applications of soap, vinegar, and water. Here is how to do it: first blot what you can with paper towels. Then mix one teaspoon of mild dishwashing liquid in one cup of warm water. Dip a clean towel in the liquid, and dab on the stain, working from the outside in. Do not overwet. Rinse with fresh water and let the area dry. Next mix one-third of a cup of white vinegar and two-thirds of a cup of water and dab on the stain. Rinse with clean water, then blot until dry. Once the area is totally dry (after at least twenty-four hours), sprinkle the entire carpet with baking soda. Vacuum up after a few hours. Dogs tend to be attracted to a spot that they have soiled in the past. Vinegar doesn't stain and it kills the odor, and the dog will not be tempted to urinate in that same spot in the future.
- Neutralize urine odors on any surface by dampening the spot and sprinkling borax over it. Rub the borax into the area and let it dry. Brush or vacuum up to remove the dry borax.
- Eliminate odors from pet beds by liberally sprinkling bedding with baking soda; wait fifteen minutes, then vacuum. Baking soda is not harmful to dogs.
- Use foaming shaving cream to remove muddy paw print stains from your carpet. Just spray it on, rub in gently, let dry, and vacuum.

will soon let you know when he needs to go out. Be sure to look for warning signs such as sniffing the floor, turning in circles, or beginning to squat. If any of these things happen, take him outside right away. If your puppy makes a mess in the house, do not punish him or rub his nose in it, as this will not change the situation or prevent another accident, and it may even set back the training process. Reinforce the proper schedule, and your puppy will soon learn what you expect of him.

Occasionally, some dogs do eat their own droppings. A good way to

Growing up with a loyal herding dog, such as an Australian Shepherd, is a life-changing, formative experience for a young child.

break this bad habit is to sprinkle a teaspoon of monosodium glutamate (MSG) over their food. This has no harmful digestive effects but makes stools inedible to your dog.

Developing the Puppy into a Well-Adjusted Adult

What makes a puppy turn into a good adult dog? Puppies that are exposed to high-quality positive experiences from an early age turn into well-adjusted adults. Every puppy needs positive reinforcement, which helps build a good foundation and the will to please. Puppies with good foundations develop the ability to cope with all kinds of people and situations.

Even if the history or temperament of your pups' parents suggests the pup may be prone to behavioral problems, and even if your pup has a bad experience when young, a good foundation gives him a better chance of developing good social skills. On the other hand, you may experience problems with puppies that are not from temperamentally sound parents no matter what you do—an important reason for buying a puppy from a reputable source. As was emphasized in the discussion of finding a reputable breeder, reputable breeders do not breed dogs that are not temperamentally sound.

Try not to put your puppy in overly stressful or potentially traumatic situations with humans during his formative early months. Early socialization and love are the keys to having a well-adjusted puppy. Socialize your puppy from the very first by handling him often. Many other practices contribute to socialization, such as talking to him, brushing him, and getting him used to the presence of and proper handling by other people. Introduce the puppy to safe new environments throughout his puppyhood and he will be well prepared to encounter new situations later in life.

One potentially stressful situation you can help your puppy deal with is a visit to the vet. Reassure your puppy that everything is under control. If you have a positive attitude, the puppy will be more relaxed and better behaved.

Dealing with Difficult Behavior

Enroll your puppy in a basic obedience class at an early age so he learns to mind you, and he'll be a pleasure to own. Even with early training, however, sometimes dogs display annoying behavior. Perhaps they dig incessantly. Perhaps they bark for no apparent reason, antagonizing the neighbors. But dogs do not misbehave because they're spiteful or are out to annoy or anger you. The fact is that dog behavioral problems that we can't stand are not problems at all to the dogs. Their misbehavior is the normal effect of two common problems, both of which you can remedy.

The first common cause of misbehavior is lack of exercise. A dog that doesn't get enough exercise tends to be hyperactive and display destructive behaviors. More exercise is only half the solution, however, as dogs need leadership as well. It's very important that you assume the role of the alpha leader from the very beginning! Developing this skill will pay off tenfold. No matter how strong-willed or submissive, dogs are innately pack animals. They instinctively need to belong to a pack because their survival in the wild depended on it. Their status in the pack is established and enforced by the alpha pack leader. The alpha dog sets the rules and maintains his position by asserting his authority when challenged.

When we bring a dog into the human–dog pack, the same pack needs apply. In this situation, the owner must become the alpha pack leader and provide rules, guidelines, and structure for the pack. Being a strong and effective leader does not mean that you are overbearing. It means learning how to communicate alpha signals all dogs will understand. The alpha pack leader will be firm and stern when a situation requires but will always be reasonable to provide a stable human–dog pack environment.

The second common cause of misbehavior is boredom. Chewing, for example, a natural teething behavior in puppies, is in older dogs often a response to boredom, separation anxiety, or undernourishment as well as a lack of exercise. Always provide plenty of chew toys as an alternative chewing outlet, especially for puppies. To control chewing, you can spray bitter apple (available at pet stores) on items you don't want chewed. Home remedies include spraying items you want your dog to stay away from with hot pepper sauce, vinegar, or alum mixed with water.

Herding breeds may chew when they get bored or when they are left alone. Chewing is often a sign that you need to spend more time with your dog. Dogs are social beings and want to be a part of your life. Obedience training is essential to reinforce the good manners you teach and model at home.

Don't leave your dog alone during thunderstorms. Many dogs completely unravel during thunderstorms. Many have been lost when they ran from their fenced yards in terror. Some dogs will throw up out of fear, and some will break out of houses, even crashing through windows or doors. Help your dog cope with the stress and fear of thunderstorms, which can get worse as a dog ages until he loses his hearing. Be sure to provide your dog with a safe place to be during storms, not outside. You might want your dog to rest in his crate until the lightning and thunder subside.

Hunger, boredom, and odor attractants can encourage dogs to dig through the trash. Store your trash can in an area inaccessible to your dog, or use a can with a sealed lid. You can spray bitter apple or some of the home remedies mentioned previously as chewing deterrents on trash cans too.

Dogs dig in the ground out of boredom or to escape the confines of a yard. Whatever the reason, discourage digging early because it is a tough habit to break.

You may be able to relieve your dog's summer boredom by partially filling a kiddie pool to help him cool off in hot weather. If you put a few toys in the pool, he can cool off and play at the same time. It is a great way to help him pass the time.

Your Dog and the Law

Dog ownership is regulated at the state or local level. In most places today, local ordinances require dog owners to keep their dog under control at all times. A dog must be on a leash outdoors, especially on public grounds such as sidewalks and city parks, and in many places your dog must be tied in your yard if it is not securely fenced. If you live on a farm or ranch, it's OK for your dog to run free (on your own private property).

Licensing and health agencies also require dogs' shots to be current. Your dog's veterinarian will tell you how often your pet needs to be wormed and when vaccinations are due. The core vaccines are distemper, parvovirus, and adenovirus 2 (usually combined in one vaccine). These are recommended at eight, ten, and twelve weeks, with a booster one year later. The rabies vaccine should be administered at fourteen weeks with a booster at one year; thereafter, follow state requirements for booster intervals, which vary from one to three years. Other optional boosters to consider may be leptovirus, Lyme disease, and Giardia. (Refer to the section on drug sensitivity in chapter 7.)

There is no way to guarantee a dog will never bite anyone. You can significantly reduce the risk by socializing your dog when he is young. Introduce your dog to many different people and situations so that he is not nervous or frightened of normal social interaction. Teach your dog appropriate behavior. Never teach your dog to chase after

Active dogs require entertainment or they become bored and destructive. A wading pool is a fun way to cool off your dog in summer months.

or attack others, even in fun. Dogs don't always understand the difference between pretend and real-life situations or threats.

If you're not sure how your dog will react to a new situation, be very cautious. If you think your dog may panic in a crowd, leave him at home. If your dog overreacts to visitors or delivery and service personnel, keep him in another room. Work with professionals to help your dog become accustomed to these and other situations. Until you are confident of his behavior, however, avoid stressful settings.

Two kinds of laws impose liability on owners. Many states have laws that make a dog owner legally liable for any injury or property damage the dog causes. More than half the states have statutes that make dog owners liable if their dog injures a person. Although commonly called dog-bite statutes, many of these laws cover all kinds of dog-inflicted injuries, not just bites. They are called "strict liability" statutes because they impose liability without fault—that is, an injured person does not have to prove that the dog owner did anything wrong. It makes no difference if the owner was careful with the dog, or didn't know he would hurt anyone, or conscientiously tried to keep him from injuring anyone. The owner of a dog that bites a person in a public place, or a person who is lawfully on private property, including the property of the owner of the dog, is liable for damages suffered by the person bitten. This is regardless of the owner's lack of knowledge of the dog's past or present viciousness.

A second type of liability involves cleaning up after your dog. Many dog owners exercise their dogs in city parks and other open spaces used by the general public. In most such places, dog owners are breaking the law if they allow their dogs to foul an area and do not clean it up. Get in the habit of carrying a poop-scoop or plastic bag with you when exercising your dog. Some parks provide bags, but it is best to bring your own (plastic grocery bags work well).

All dog owners and the parents of small children should understand the importance of cleaning up after their dogs. The excrement of dogs that are not regularly wormed or vaccinated can contain the eggs of *Toxocara canis*, a parasitic

Provide appropriate chew toys for the growing puppy, or he'll discover his own teething objects.

roundworm also known as dog roundworm that is often present in pregnant bitches and young puppies. *T. canis* can infect humans as well as dogs, causing toxocariasis, an eye disease that can lead to blindness. Toddlers and young children are most at risk, as they often play on the ground and put their fingers in their mouths. Disposing of dog droppings is an important way to stop the spread of toxocariasis. And besides, no one likes to step in poop, so it's nice when people are considerate and clean up after their dogs.

Chasing sheep, outmaneuvering cow hooves, and staring down wayward goats burn a lot of calories in your average herding dog. Feeding working dogs requires the best possible food and lots of it.

Chapter

4

Feeding and Grooming the Active Herding Dog

Feeding your herding dog high-quality food will help keep him healthy. How can you tell if the food you are feeding is high quality? The dog's coat will be shiny, plush, and resilient. You can also tell by your dog's attitude. If he has energy, loves to run and play, and seems content, these are all signs of a healthy diet. Dogs need a complete and balanced diet that contains fats, proteins, carbohydrates, vitamins, and minerals in the correct proportions for optimal growth and development.

Growing puppies and adolescents need more calories, plus protein and nutrients, than same-size adult dogs do.

Most dogs eat enough to satisfy their energy needs. Use the recommendations on the product label as a guideline to ensure you are not under- or overfeeding your dog. The average adult dog needs one or two meals a day. Puppies less than three months old need three or four daily feedings, and senior dogs need their daily requirements divided into several smaller meals. Pregnant and lactating dogs may require multiple feedings or dietary supplements.

Proper Diet Depends on a Dog's Age and Activity

Each stage of a dog's life has different nutritional requirements. Puppies need a diet high in protein, fat, vitamins, and minerals to support their rapid growth. Lactating dogs have similar requirements. Young dogs in growth stages require two and a half times the caloric intake of an adult in the maintenance stage. Adult or maintenance diets are formulated to maintain the weight of an average adult dog and are suitable for pregnant dogs until they start nursing their puppies. For less active or overweight adult dogs there are light formulas, and obese dogs may need specifically designed weight-reduction diets available from your vet. Senior foods for the older dog contain less fat and fewer calories in line with their slower metabolism but extra vitamins and minerals to maintain their health.

Avoid feeding table scraps to your dog, as food scraps are not nutritionally balanced and can lead to poor skin and coat, allergies, dietary intolerance, obesity, and other health problems. Feeding table scraps also encourages begging. It has been said that to a dog, food and love amount to the same thing. You must be careful not to equate the two, and make the difference clear to your dog. Just like you, your dog must eat to live: don't feed him to make him love you. If you train your dog with goodies and food, he will respond to these and not to your care. The result of this can be life-threatening to your dog. Food should never be a substitute for care, petting, and company.

Begging is not an easy habit to break. It's very disturbing when you are trying to eat and your dog is drooling on you and your guests to get what he can out of the meal. Dogs who beg will do almost anything to get what they want. They whine, bark, drool, and even snatch the food if they get a chance. As the owner of a dog, it's up to you to decide what behaviors are unacceptable. Address a begging problem immediately and firmly: if you are the right kind of owner,

The dog's food bowl should contain all the nourishment the dog requires for a day or half day. Avoid free-feeding or supplementing with table scraps.

your dog will realize you're in charge, and he will obey to please you. Don't wait until the habit is entrenched or out of control.

A herding dog's activities also determine his dietary needs. A working dog, or a dog that participates in high-energy performance events, requires a diet that is higher in fat than the diets of less active dogs. Finally, an adult dog's nutritional requirements can vary depending on breed, environment, temperament, and stress factors.

Choosing Commercial Dog Food

When it comes to commercial dog food, you get what you pay for. Premium pet foods made by reputable companies are high in quality and have a fixed ingredient profile or recipe. This means that the ingredients and their proportions are exactly the same in each batch, and they are made according to higher manufacturing standards. Cheaper brands use less expensive ingredients. The result is an inconsistent and poorer quality product that can be detrimental to your dog's health, causing poor skin and coat condition, less energy, or loose stools.

Store your dog food in a dry, cool place to extend its freshness. If you decide to switch brands, make the change gradually in your dog's food bowl over the course of about a week. Start by adding a small amount of the new food to the old food, gradually increasing the new food and decreasing the current food proportion at each feeding. If you change from one food to another all at once, your dog may get diarrhea.

Look on the back of the bag for the "Guaranteed Analysis." This tells you the amount of each essential nutrient the food contains. It will list the amount of crude protein, crude fat, crude fiber, moisture, vitamins such as A and E, minerals, and omega-6 and omega-3 fatty acids. Many foods will also contain glucosamine hydrochloride and chondroitin sulfate, which are recommended to help your adult dog maintain healthy joint cartilage. In addition to the guaranteed analysis, you will find the calorie content and ingredients, which are important to consider because although the guaranteed analysis lists the minimum or maximum amounts of crude protein, fat, moisture, fiber, and ash that are contained in the food, the analysis does not guarantee the digestibility of the ingredients.

Just like ingredient lists on people-food packaging, ingredients listed on dog-food bags are in decreasing order by weight or percentage. The first three ingredients are the ones to pay the most attention to. Look for foods that list meat (not by-products) at the top. Make sure the food you choose contains chicken, beef, or lamb. The ideal protein source should be fresh meat, which means the product will be easy to digest. Foods that primarily contain by-products such as ground chicken beaks, feet, and even feathers are of lesser quality and lack proper nutrition. Chicken meal, lamb meal, and beef meal are OK listed as the second or third ingredient.

Perhaps the most important consideration when selecting the right food for your dog is the taste. If your dog eats it with gusto, you're in business.

Lots of dog-food companies use rice in their recipes. Rice is fine unless your dog has an allergic reaction to it. Stay away from dog food that lists corn as the first or second ingredient; it may be less expensive, but it is lower in quality, and many dogs have adverse reactions to corn. Look for fresh ingredients. Potatoes, carrots, peas, flaxseed, dried apples, and cranberries are all fine ingredients (all are carbohydrates dogs need for optimal health), as long as they are not among the first three ingredients on the label. Ultimately, the label can only tell you so much; it cannot guarantee the quality of the individual ingredients. A more detailed list of the various ingredients is usually unavailable because most manufacturers consider their exact recipes proprietary information.

In general, a balanced dog food contains approximately 23% crude protein and 14–23% crude fat. Adequate protein is essential; it provides amino acids, the building blocks with which the body performs vital functions and rebuilds its tissues.

Fats are a good concentrated source of energy—vital to herding dogs—which expend a lot of energy. The diet for active herding dogs should include at least 15% fat. Fats are necessary for the absorption of fat-soluble vitamins and are a source of essential unsaturated fatty acids. Fat also improves the palatability (taste) and digestibility of food. Adequate dietary fat also helps maintain a dog's healthy coat.

Fiber is also important in the diet, as it helps maintain gastrointestinal health.

Minerals in dog food are important for normal regulatory functions in the body. The macro minerals (calcium, phosphorus, potassium, sodium, and magnesium) make up the bulk of dietary minerals, but micro minerals (iron, zinc, copper, manganese, iodine, and selenium) are equally essential for a dog's normal body functions.

Vitamins promote and regulate various physiological processes. They are divided into two groups: fat-soluble (A, D, E, and K) and water-soluble (thiamine, riboflavin, niacin, pantothenic acid, folic acid, vitamin B6, choline, and vitamin B12).

Dog food is sold in three forms: dry, soft-moist, and canned. Dry dog food is the most popular and usually the most economical choice, and it has the advantage of reducing the buildup of tartar on the dog's

Serving Amounts

Refer to the feeding chart on the back of each bag of dog food for recommended serving amounts. The following portion guide is widely accepted as the industry standard (essentially ½– 1 cup for every ten pounds):

½ – 1 cup	for dogs/puppies weighing ten pounds or less
1 – 1 ½ cups	for dogs weighing ten to twenty pounds
1 ½ – 2 cups	for dogs weighing twenty to thirty pounds
2 – 2 ½ cups	for dogs weighing thirty to forty pounds
2 ½ – 3 ⅓ cups	for dogs weighing forty to sixty pounds
3 ⅓ – 4 cups	for dogs weighing sixty to eighty pounds
4 – 4 ½ cups	for dogs weighing eighty to 100 pounds

teeth. Most dogs do very well on dry dog food as long as they have plenty of fresh clean water to drink.

Feed a good-quality food to help your dog maintain a healthy weight, skin, and hair. If his skin is clear without any flakes or scales and his coat is shiny, not dull or brittle, then the food you are feeding is good. Generally, the more expensive foods go through more rigorous testing, and the protein used in it is of a higher standard.

Generally, you can buy high-quality (albeit more expensive) dog foods through veterinary offices, feed stores, and pet stores. In general, stay away from dog food sold in grocery stores. Foods sold in grocery stores are less expensive and of lesser quality. The brands of dog food sold in grocery stores are usually made with large amounts of corn and usually large amounts of salt and by-products.

The higher quality proteins and fats used in premium foods make them highly palatable and digestible. Premium brands are significantly higher in nutritional density, meaning you feed much smaller amounts, the bag lasts longer, and your dog should produce a smaller stool.

Raw meat, fish, and poultry is not recommended for your dog, as they can contain bacteria, toxins, and parasites that are normally destroyed in the cooking process. Chicken bones are particularly dangerous because they can splinter and cause internal damage.

Food Allergies

Food allergies account for about 10% of all the allergies seen in dogs. There is no strong link between food allergies and specific breeds. Food allergies can show up as early as five months and as late as twelve years of age, although the vast majority of cases occur between two and six years. Dogs with food allergies also have concurrent inhalant or contact allergies.

In dogs, food allergies result in diarrhea or vomiting, in contrast to the typical food allergy reactions in people such as hives and respiratory distress. Food intolerances in pets would be similar to people who get diarrhea or an upset stomach from eating spicy or fried foods. Fortunately, both food intolerances and allergies can be eliminated with a diet free from offending agents. Several studies have shown that some ingredients are more likely to

Never Feed Your Dog Chocolate

Poisoning of dogs by chocolate is not as uncommon as you might think. Chocolate contains a stimulant found in the cocoa bean, theobromine. It naturally increases urination and affects the central nervous system as well as the heart muscle. While amounts of this chemical vary by type of chocolate, theobromine in all chocolates is poisonous to dogs. The lethal dose of theobromine depends on the size of the dog and the type of chocolate. Ounce for ounce, baking chocolate has six to nine times more theobromine than milk chocolate. While a very small amount of chocolate may not harm some dogs, it's safest to avoid giving it to them at all. If accidental ingestion occurs, a veterinarian should be consulted.

Within a few hours of eating the chocolate, symptoms begin, including vomiting, diarrhea, and hyperactivity. As time passes and more theobromine is metabolized, the dog's heart rate increases, which can cause arrhythmia, restlessness, hyperactivity, muscle twitching, increased urination, or excessive panting. This can lead to hyperthermia, muscle tremors, seizures, coma, and even death.

Treatment may require inducing vomiting, stabilizing the dog's heartbeat and respiration, controlling seizures, and slowing the absorption of theobromine. If the dog is comatose, his stomach may need to be pumped.

cause food allergies than others. The most common offenders in dogs, in descending order, are beef, dairy products, chicken, wheat, chicken eggs, corn, and soy. As you may have noticed, the most common offenders are the most common ingredients in dog foods.

Veterinarians sometimes recommend that a dog suspected of having a food allergy only needs to be placed on a special diet for three weeks. New studies show, however, that only 26% of dogs with food allergies responded by day twenty-one, while the vast majority of pets responded by twelve weeks. Therefore, it is very important to keep the pet on the diet for the entire twelve weeks. If the dog shows a marked reduction or elimination of symptoms, the animal is placed back on the original food. This is called provocative testing, and it is essential to confirm the diagnosis. If the symptoms return after going back on the original diet, the diagnosis of a food allergy is confirmed. If there has been no change in symptoms but a food allergy is still strongly suspected, then another food trial using a different novel food source could be tried.

Once you have a positive diagnosis, the treatment is very straightforward. The owner of the animal has two choices: feed the animal a special commercially prepared diet, or feed him a homemade diet.

Grooming

There is almost as wide an assortment of coats in herding dogs as there are categories of dogs. Most have weather-resistant double coats of all lengths and from medium to hard textures. As you would expect, there are differences between the kind of grooming a working stockdog requires and the grooming techniques used on dogs being shown in a conformation ring. The following grooming advice is intended to keep a non–show dog healthy and free from debris that would cause the dog discomfort or injury.

Regardless of the coat type or length, herding dogs should never be shaved. Shaving the coat leaves the skin vulnerable to sunburn and scrapes and scratches. In the heat of summer, you can help your dog be more comfortable by brushing out the undercoat and thinning out long outer hair if you own one of the longer-coated breeds.

A long double coat will require a wire slicker brush to keep it maintained. Purchase the best quality grooming tools you can find. They'll last a lifetime.

Clean coats are healthy coats. Brushing is one of the best ways to keep the hair coat free of debris. Herding dogs used for working in pastures and in fields are more likely to pick up grass awns (wild oat seeds, foxtails) and other debris that can filter through the coat and eventually into the skin. To keep this debris from becoming embedded, he should be brushed several times a week. Regular grooming also keeps dogs' skin free from parasites and fungal and bacterial infections. Regular bathing is also desirable for most breeds.

Although short-coated breeds don't require extensive grooming, it's best to introduce puppies to the basics at a young age.

Other grooming practices you can perform to keep your dog healthy include cleaning the ear leather with mild ear-cleaning solution and trimming toenails and dewclaws. Canine dental care is as important as human dental care is. Some owners prefer to brush their dog's teeth with a toothbrush and toothpaste designed specifically for pets. If dogs are given an appropriate diet supplemented with proper chew bones, they may only need to have their teeth scaled occasionally with a scaling tool.

Grooming the Different Coat Types

Most of the herding breeds' coats need regular brushing with some exceptions; the coats that are flocked or corded have special requirements. Grooming is an important part of a dog's health. Regular brushing and combing help remove dead hair and dirt and prevent matting. Dogs that get groomed regularly tend to have a healthier and shinier coat because it stimulates the blood supply to the skin.

Grooming a dog is so much more than just making the coat look nice and shiny. Grooming can also be a good way to bond with your dog, and it's important to get him used to it from an early age. Many dogs learn to see their routine brushing as an alternate petting, another source of affection.

Smooth Coat: Smooth-coated breeds are the easiest to care for. An occasional bath and a good brushing is all that is needed.

Double Coat: The undercoat in a double-coated breed is usually influenced by climatic conditions and individual breed characteristics. These dogs should be brushed thoroughly on a regular basis to remove dead undercoat.

Corded Coat: Bathing a corded coat might be described as washing a fine quality sweater. Pour diluted low-lathering shampoo over the coat and gently massage cords, taking care not to rub. Rubbing can cause the coat to break at the base. Once the shampoo mixture has been gently squeezed into the cords and worked over the entire body, then you can rinse the coat with clean lukewarm water, repeating the process and squeezing clean water into the cords until the water runs clear.

A handy grooming tool is the two-sided brush, including a bristle brush and a pin brush. Both types of brushes are useful on medium- and long-coated dogs.

Curly Coat: Curly-coated dogs must be brushed prior to bathing, as debris easily gets trapped as the wet coat tightens up. Break up mats gently prior to bathing.

Keep your dog's nails short and even to avoid the feet becoming splayed or the nails getting ripped on furniture, wood flooring, or clothing.

All coats must be completely dried after a bath so moisture doesn't become trapped next to the skin, causing irritation.

Excess hair should be trimmed away from around the paws so mud and other debris cannot ball up. The hair between pads can be neatened up, but not so much as to expose the webbing. The front feathers or rear britches should be trimmed or thinned out on any dog if debris or excrement gets entangled in the hair.

Use absorbent towels to gently squeeze out excess water. A dryer with a cool setting can be used along with plenty of absorbent towels to blot extra moisture.

Trim to tidy up the feet and any area around the rear end to keep debris (excrement) from being trapped.

One of the most interesting coat types is that of the Bergamasco, which is made up of three types of hair—undercoat, "goat hair," and outer coat. The undercoat is short, dense, and of fine texture, oily to the touch and forming a waterproof layer against the skin. The goat hair is long, straight, and rough in texture. The outer coat is wooly and somewhat finer in texture than the goat hair. Goat hair is limited to breeds that have flocked/corded coats.

Grooming the Bergamasco is completely different from grooming herding breeds with other coat types. In breeds with coat types that are not flocked or corded, matting is not considered a positive feature. In this case, it is the breed's pride and glory—a coat is full of heavy matting that almost looks unmanageable.

The coat of the Bergamasco does not need brushing or combing, particularly when young, as the flocks must form. Sometimes in the early stages of flock development, the puppy hair can mat close to the skin. These areas must be separated by hand, as though true flocks are taking shape, so the skin is not pulled. As the Bergamasco nears its first birthday, coarser goat hair and fuzzy "wool" begin to appear, at which point the coat must be split or "ripped" into mats. This process of separating the hair into sections can take a few hours or at most a few evenings, but once it is done, it's done for life. For the next six months, a weekly check to make sure the mats have not grown back together is all that is required. After that, the mats stay separate and become dense enough that very few things get caught in them. Once fully flocked, the Bergamasco's coat requires very little care other than occasional brushing and bathing.

A corded coat may seem intimidating at first, but owners find that these coats require surprisingly minimal effort to maintain.

The only way a herding dog can train to move a thousand head of sheep is through experience. The seasonal migration of herds is the Olympics of herding dogs.

Chapter
5

Training the Herding Dog

Instinct tests determine whether or not a dog has a strong basic working instinct. The American Herding Breed Association (AHBA) and American Kennel Club (AKC) sponsor instinct tests that are run by certified instinct testers who have experience with at least the breed being tested and often other breeds as well.

Instinct Tests and Training

Young and insecure dogs may show little or no interest on their first introduction to instinct tests, but they should definitely be retested at a later date. In some cases, it can take

Herding Dog Terms and Commands

Away-to-me:	Counterclockwise movement in relation to the flock.
Bark:	Woof, yap, a herding dog barks as a means of showing power.
Bite:	Sink teeth into, nip, snap. Nipping or gripping at the bodies of sheep or cattle. A bite or a nip at livestock as a means to move or control stubborn stock.
Bring 'em in:	Dog gathers livestock without direction from his handler.
Come-bye:	Clockwise movement in relation to the flock.
Drive:	Moving the stock from behind; when a dog pushes stock in a forward direction.
Drove:	To drive groups of livestock moving forward.
Easy:	Directs the dog to approach the flock or move around the flock more slowly.
Eye:	An intense gaze used by the dog to control stock. Watching and staring down the stock. This is a characteristic of many working dogs which allows control over the livestock.
Gather:	To collect, assemble, draw together, bunch up livestock.
Get around:	Sends the dog out to gather livestock.
Get back:	Tells the dog to move away from the livestock.
Get out:	A reprimand; the dog is too close to the flock.
Lie down:	The dog should stop, not necessarily lie down.
Lift:	The very first movement of the stock; also, the moment between the outrun and start of the fetch.
Look back:	Directs the dog to move back and gather animals that may have split from the rest of the flock.
Mustering:	Gathering together.
Stop them at the head:	To bring to a halt at the head of the animal being herded.
That'll do:	Directs the dog to stop working and return to the handler.
Tending:	Keeping a watchful eye over, paying attention to.
Walk-up:	Get up; move closer to the flock.

repeated exposures to stir up the herding instincts.

Once a dog has been introduced to stock and exhibits the desire to work, the next step is to begin training to develop his skills for practical work around the farm or in trial competition.

Herding clinics are helpful, as they give new handlers hands-on instruction in the most effective methods of training their dogs. During these sessions, the handler is taught a basic understanding of proper livestock-handling techniques. Clinics are a good place to introduce dogs to stock in a safe and controlled environment. The first introduction to livestock must be carefully supervised. Training can start once the handler understands how livestock moves away from pressure points and the dog has shown confidence around stock.

Regardless of breed, training the young dog in basic obedience can be advantageous to the handler prior to introducing a dog to stock. It is imperative that your dog comes when he is called and responds to stop (stand, sit, or lie down) commands. Without these basic commands, you will have little or no control over your dog, and you will surely be unable to work as a team or successfully manage the stock. Teaching obedience is the one thing you can do for yourself. It pays off, for a dog that listens is a pleasure to be around.

Early Training

Contrary to the opinion of some, a herding dog that is a family companion and pet can also become an excellent worker. Having children play with the family dog or letting people pet him does not make him a poor candidate for herding training. Improper training or weak discipline on the handler's part, however, can affect a dog's ability to listen.

The young herding dog that enthusiastically plays fetch can grow up into a reliable working and trial dog.

When the dog is young, there are things you can do that will facilitate the training process. As the young dog shows an inclination to play with a ball or toy, start using the commands (words and whistle signals) that you will use later on stock. While some good herding dogs do not play ball, the very best trial dogs will. You can teach a puppy to bring the ball back to you from every direction in which you throw it. When he reaches the ball, say "fetch" and repeat the word as many times as necessary to reinforce its meaning in his mind. When he reaches you, encourage him to give up the ball and give him much praise and attention.

When the young dog has the fetch command firmly in mind, throw the ball, this time saying "fetch" when he reaches it while also giving a long, low-pitched whistle signal to come in. Each trainer needs to work out the signals he or she prefers and use them consistently.

This fetching game should be continued only as long as the dog shows interest, preferably not more than ten or so minutes at a time. More than that and you risk dampening the dog's enthusiasm. It is important to make this early stage of training fun.

The most important command in herding work is the command to stop. This skill will help the handler gain control when necessary. This signal can be given with a quick short burst on a whistle. The dog can be taught to respond to the verbal command "stand" or "lie down," whichever you prefer.

Another way the ball can be used to prepare the dog for real work is to throw the ball to the dog and then, when the dog catches the ball, ask him to stop and hold that position momentarily. Use a low steady whistle command to tell the dog to bring the ball back to you steadily. If the dog starts too fast, stop him, then ask him to come on steady. This can be used when you teach the dog to move toward the sheep in a steady, easy manner. You can also use the command "steady" or "easy" to persuade the dog to walk to you with the ball or toy. If the dog attempts to race back to you, stop him and then reissue the command "steady." Your dog will soon learn what each command means.

A key component in any herding dog is its alertness and willingness to pay attention to its human master. This puppy has returned the tennis ball and is waiting for another command.

Types of Herding

Most types of herding dogs are similar in that they are agile, alert, and extremely athletic. They are intelligent dogs, bred to work effectively under a wide variety of circumstances and in different ways, depending on the breed.

Boundary-Style Herding

Most herding breeds are capable of holding stock within a specified grazing area. Because they are naturally territorial, they can easily learn to distinguish boundaries and to keep the flock within or away from certain areas.

Tending involves grazing flocks under the supervision of a shepherd and dog, in both Europe and the American West. Tending is a method of keeping livestock from crossing a boundary (flock containment). A common practice in Germany and

This Australian Shepherd instinctively knows the territorial bounds of his flock and will keep the sheep within their area.

This dog demonstrates keeping the flock moving as a tight unit as he works with the author's son Vincent.

certain parts of Europe, tending is often referred to as boundary work. In boundary-style herding, the flock is taken out along roads, past unfenced fields, to grazing areas such as a field or land being rested from crop production. The flock is also grazed in unfenced pastures or fields bordered by crops that could be destroyed by a flock if they were not prevented from grazing and trampling down the crops.

The dogs used for this type of work have the ability to work close to the flock and do their job forcefully. Sheep are allowed to graze the grass strips between the row crops, and dogs are responsible for prohibiting the sheep from damaging the crops. The denser the population and the greater the crop acreage, the more controlled the usage of grazing areas must be. In some areas, the sheep are kept in a compact group and required to thoroughly graze the specific vicinity before being moved to an adjacent area. The herder indicates the boundary to the dogs, and the dogs prohibit the sheep from going beyond these limits, hence the name "boundary herding."

Not until the American Kennel Club developed the herding program was this style of herding seen in the United States. Sheep on the American Western ranges were not as closely supervised as the sheep are in the more populated and cultivated plains of Europe. Usually in the tundra or the mountains, flocks are allowed to spread out more; the close grazing practiced in the cultivated areas of France and Germany would be too intense for the vegetation there.

Droving

"Droving" is sometimes confused with "driving," leading to the thought that a dog described in old accounts as a "droving" dog must have had particular instincts to "drive" the animals out ahead of the

A large flock requires a sheepdog with greater control of the flock to keep them in their proper grazing area.

This determined herder clearly demonstrates his "strong eye" and control of his bovine charge.

handler, as opposed to "fetching." However, this is not the case. Droving meant taking the stock some distance, down roads or lanes, usually to market.

Working Styles

The instinct and desire to keep the flock together is inherited. One animal may split off, but herding instincts will urge the untrained dog to put it back with the others and keep the bunch together. The herding dog's ability to manage livestock depends on his presence and power over his charges. Bark, bite, and eye are three important ways herding dogs assert power.

The main difference between herding breeds is how they use "eye." A strong eye can be seen in the Border Collie. "Strong eye" means that a dog uses an intent gaze, like a cat on the hunt, as he works the stock, approaching with the head dropped in a stalking manner.

Loose-eyed dogs, on the other hand, generally work with their heads up in an upright posture, using

Top: When the "eye" fails, the voice delivers the message directly. Barking reinforces the herding dog's directives. Bottom: Demonstrating the "medium eye," this Border Collie approaches his charge with the intensity and posture of a wolf stalking its prey. No wonder sheep see and obey!

their bodies for controlling the stock through blocking movements more than eye. They tend to push right up to the stock with little apparent concern for the flight zone. These types of herding dogs take in the whole picture.

Individuals of generally loose-eyed breeds may show varying degrees of eye. Medium-eyed dogs use eye only for power. They approach steadily with their heads slightly lowered using eye contact, as a wolf stalks its prey. When they no longer need to exert power, they relax to conserve energy.

Using voice or a bark can be at times more effective than eye, especially for urging large numbers of stock. Voice without authority and continual barking can be distracting and irritating, however, and a hindrance instead of a help. Continual barking is often a sign of an inexperienced dog or a lack of confidence.

A correct bark or bite is often necessary to move ornery or stubborn stock. When stocks get "sticky" and don't want to move, some dogs bark to urge them on. Barking can be beneficial in certain situations. For example, when sheep jam up at a narrow passage, it is desirable for the dog to bark to help shift the flock, or even to jump onto the backs of the leaders to move them.

At dinnertime, you can teach your dog to use his voice with a piece of food by asking the dog to "speak" for his treat. Practice this once or twice, but don't overdo it. While teaching the dog to bark, you should also teach the dog to stop barking with "that's enough" or an equivalent command.

There are times when a bite correctly placed is acceptable. The dog has been taught to be gentle with sheep and ducks, but he must learn more assertive methods of herding cattle or hogs. Bite or grip may be necessary to manage cattle, hogs, and unruly sheep. Body biting is not appropriate, and it is sometimes the sign of a young, inexperienced dog or one lacking suitable instincts. Nipping should only be used when needed, and preferably on the heels of cows below the hock or dewclaws or on the face, nose, or poll of the head.

Basic Stockdog Training Skills

There are many methods of training. A herding dog may respond better to one technique than another, and

On the move, this Belgian Tervuren is fetching three goats toward the shepherd.

no one training technique is perfect. In training a herding dog, it is best to work with the dog's natural ability. Find a training method that works, and fine-tune the process according to the animal's unique characteristics.

Most dogs are ready to begin light training between nine and eighteen months of age. It is a common practice to focus on gathering or fetching first. This is because, for many dogs, gathering work helps develop balance and the ability to independently cover the moves of the stock. If a dog's gathering ability is weak, the dog will not have developed the skills necessary to control the stock.

Stock training should start in a small pen that is about 90 to 100 feet in diameter. The first introduction to stock should be a safe and positive experience for the dog. You will need a small group (five to ten head) of gentle sheep, goats, or ducks to begin with. Don't use stubborn or untamed sheep or ducks that have been overworked and soured by dogs. Cattle can be used for training if they are available, but only if you are certain they are gentle.

As discussed earlier, basic obedience training is a major key to herding success. Make sure your dog knows the stop signal before turning him loose on the livestock. The stop signal must be obeyed so the handler is in control at all times. Most dogs do not readily obey when first being introduced to stock. It will be less frustrating for the handler if the dog stops when you want him to and comes when called. Once you have practiced this and the dog understands the signal to stop, you are ready to continue.

Allow the dog to move around the flock under supervision and to try to keep the animals together. A dog with good instincts will naturally bring the sheep, ducks, or goats toward you. Give the fetch command so the dog will associate it with gathering and bringing the stock toward you. He will soon get the idea of fetching. Move backward while still facing the livestock, and continue encouraging your dog to move toward the stock. Expect the dog's movements to be disorganized at first; some human guidance will

Stock training best occurs in a small pen with a cooperative cow. Avoid using stressed or weary livestock that may challenge the canine apprentice.

Moving a paddle of reluctant ducks, this Border Collie gets behind his anatine charges to keep them waddling forward.

be necessary to help the dog keep the stock calmly moving together in one group. If the livestock gets split up, regroup them. Give the dog time to settle down, and then resume gathering.

It's common for an inexperienced dog with a very strong desire to go to the head of the livestock to "stop them at the head." This means the dog ends up holding the animals to the fence. Not all herding dogs demonstrate the same gathering or driving tendencies. Some are better at one or the other, and some show tendencies for both gathering and driving. Some dogs show a definite preference for driving by deliberately attempting to push the animals away from the trainer while keeping them grouped.

The tamer the livestock, the closer they tolerate most dogs working them. If the livestock stop or are reluctant to stay together in one group, the dog will need to go behind them. He will need to move from right to left and left to right behind them, urging them to get moving again. If the dog doesn't check himself behind the stock but wants to circle completely around, then you, the trainer, must push him back behind the stock with a training stick. As the dog moves back and forth from end to end, the stock will zigzag as you back away from the sheep being fetched or pushed to you.

Train in short sessions. Ten minutes is adequate, and several sessions can be conducted in a day. Soon the dog will be following you while continuing to bring the stock along. Remember to stop the dog occasionally while you face the dog from the other side of the flock. Let the dog and animals rest a minute, then ask him to follow again. As soon as the dog learns to steadily but slowly move the sheep to you, you can stop facing him and walking backward; instead, you can walk normally ahead, facing forward.

When the sheep resists, the dog may have to use some fancy footwork and mouthwork, although nipping must always be discouraged.

If the dog attempts to bite the livestock, correct it with a sharp "No!" You can at this point stop the dog with a sharp whistle blast. If the dog either doesn't respond or continues to try to bite, you can tap the training stick on the ground and force the dog to move back out away from the stock while also giving the command to back out. This is another lesson that can be reinforced using a ball or toy.

Make sure you keep moving ahead of the stock and are not standing in the way. Otherwise, you are hindering the stock from being able to move freely away from the dog, which can cause the dog to grab. A dog that is especially rough and wants to constantly grip may need to be muzzled for a session or two. It is important to properly fit muzzles so as not to hinder the dog's breathing. It is also critical that on warm days the muzzle be used only for short periods to prevent causing heat exhaustion.

Never drive (dog and handler follow the sheep together) before the dog clearly understands fetching. Otherwise, the dog could be ruined and will not have the correct foundation for handling stock out in open unfenced areas and in the trial arena. Until then, have the dog bring the sheep or ducks while you walk ahead wherever you go.

Training for Herding

Sending the Dog to Gather

This is when you send your dog to go out and around and bring animals to the handler, sometimes called fetching. You can practice gathering by sending the dog from your side in an arc to the opposite side of the flock from where you are standing. Begin this stage of training by fetching the stock for several minutes to quiet them down. Stop and leave them standing out in the middle of the pen or field, not against a fence. Take the dog approximately fifteen feet away from the flock. Ask the dog to stand or lie down, then walk several feet toward the sheep, stop, and face the dog.

Extend your training stick to the side opposite where you want the dog to go. In this case, you are using the training stick not to point but to block. If the dog clearly understands the fetch command to go to the stock, then it will be fairly easy to encourage him to go toward the open side (the one without the interference of the stick).

Always practice gathering the flock in the middle of a field so that the flock doesn't get backed into fencing and become upset.

When practicing penning, be sure to stay out of the stock's way so that they can keep moving and away from the dog—in this case, a Standard Schnauzer.

Some dogs require that you run with them around the flock. Never try to send the dog from too far a distance from the sheep, or he may cut in and go the wrong way. If the dog fails to circle around to the other side but cuts in instead, call him back and try again. You can also practice sending the dog to one side first, and after he learns the skill, begin sending the dog to the other side.

When the dog ends up on the opposite side of you and the flock, give a short blast on your whistle to signal for him to stop. Give verbal praise to indicate that you are pleased, but don't encourage the dog to leave his position. Hesitate briefly, then ask the dog to bring the sheep to you. The moment of hesitation is called the "lift." Lifting the flock should be done in a calm, steady manner. If the dog lifts the flock too fast, it can split the stock rather than keep them quietly together. This can become a bad habit to break. It is essential to use livestock that move freely away from the dog rather than challenge him, as stubborn

While working the flock, the apprentice herder will appreciate words of praise, but don't overdo it or the dog may relinquish his position and the flock may scatter.

stock will be difficult for dog in training to handle. After the livestock move away from the dog, your dog should fetch or bring them to you as you have practiced. If the livestock stop, the dog may need to go behind to get them going again.

With each new session, don't forget to review the previous lessons. Always end each lesson with something the dog does well to keep him looking forward to another session.

Keeping the flock together is one of the basic responsibilities of herding dogs.

Driving a herd of cows or flock of sheep requires a completely different set of skills than gathering and fetching do.

DRIVING

When the dog is proficient at going around to the head and gathering the stock and bringing them to the trainer again and again, it is time to expand the herding lesson to include driving. If you have taught your dog to stay with you when asked, you will be able to teach the drive.

Take your flock to a fenced area, training pen, or pasture. First, send the dog to gather the stock from the pasture. When this has been accomplished, call the dog to you and walk toward the animals with the dog at your side. Together, drive the stock for some distance along the fence. If the dog tries to run to the head and turn them back, stop him and call him back behind with the command "Come behind" or "Come here." Praise him for responding and continue driving. Drive the livestock to a pen or corner of the field and congratulate him for a job well done.

Training your dog to drive requires patience, because this skill goes against everything you have taught him until now. But the results will be well worth the work.

Herding trials continue to grow in popularity around the world. Whether the trial is held for a crowd of enthusiastic spectators or solely for the participants, the dogs enjoy the outlet to show off their natural skills.

Chapter
6

Herding Trials

An excellent outlet for the high-energy herding dog is the herding test or trial. These competitive and noncompetitive performance events, usually sponsored by a major sheepdog association or kennel club, attract owners of working farm or ranch dogs with substantial training, hobby herders who work their dogs on a limited or weekend basis but do not necessarily live in a farm or ranch setting, and families whose pets have little or no herding experience. The awareness of herding activities is on the increase across the United States since the inception of the American Kennel Club's (AKC) Herding Trial Program in 1989.

First, a little background on these exciting and challenging trials is in order. Sheepdog trials are the oldest type of competition for herding dogs. The first sheepdog trials were held in north Wales to the south of the Scottish Highlands in 1873 to test the skills required to work sheep in the Highlands. The trials governed by the International Sheepdog Society in Great Britain (ISDS) are sometimes called open sheepdog trials, or Border Collie trials, named after the breed that traditionally dominates them.

In the United States, sheepdog trials date back to 1880. Trials approved by the United States Border Collie Handler's Association (USBCHA) are closely patterned after the International Sheepdog Society trials. Open sheepdog trials are open to any breed capable of handling the work. Most of the loose-eyed herding breeds, however, were not developed to handle a small number of light (highly responsive) sheep at great distances. Consequently, other organizations designed programs that are better suited to the different herding styles.

In general, a herding trial comprises a series of challenging situations and tasks that a dog must complete in a specified way. The way a dog successfully completes a trial is not necessarily the same way you would want the dog to do it in a real-life situation.

Arena trials are designed to accommodate the majority of herding breeds. These trials are held in a fenced area with assorted course designs to simulate conditions on a small farm. Both the AKC and the Australian Shepherd Club of America (ASCA) hold arena trials governed by a set of rules and regulations. Trial judges look for a dog's ability and desire to keep the stock grouped together and control stock movement. For a dog to score well in a trial, he must move the stock in a controlled fashion from one end of the course to the other and respond to the handler's commands. The runs are scored according to specific criteria determined by the sponsoring organization.

When you attend a trial, you can examine dogs of many herding breeds in action. Diverse types of stock will be worked including ducks, cattle, and sheep, and it is not unusual to see the same dog work all three types of stock the same day. You'll also get invaluable demonstrations of herding dogs' different working styles: the different ways a dog gathers the stock and brings it to the handler or pushes

The close bond between a shepherd and his dog is illustrated in a long day of hard work on the Hartnagle ranch as well as in relaxing moments like this one.

the stock away, which breeds bark and which work silently. Different herding breeds use different points of balance to control the movement and direction of the livestock.

Training and Trainers

The increasing number of people participating in instinct tests has led to greater interest in herding trials and training as well as a greater number of herding dog owners who would like to compete one day in an actual trial competition. The demand for more trainers has grown accordingly. In looking for a trainer, you may discover that some trainers work with only specific breeds. If any trainer is disparaging toward your breed or dog, steer clear. It is important for both you and your dog to work with a trainer whom you feel good about.

A good place to start your search for a herding trainer is by asking the people you meet at trials. Trial organizers and participants are often excellent resources. They can recommend both classes and trainers as well as answer your general questions. Learn as much as you can about herding by reading books, attending clinics, taking herding lessons, and observing successful handlers at trials before getting started.

To find a reputable trainer, you can contact a regional or national breed club and inquire about local herding clubs. More than likely these clubs will have information about events in your area and can give you names of people who can help you.

Although your primary concern may be to find a trainer you like, find out also if he or she has experience in the type of training you are interested in. Ideally, your trainer will be experienced in training dogs for practical farm and ranch work as well as for trial competition. A good trainer will allow a young dog every possible opportunity for his natural instincts to surface.

There is a difference between dogs trained to respond to basic obedience around the house and competitive obedience dogs. There is also a difference between practical farm work and competing in a working trial. A person using a dog for simple farm chores may require only basic training. If you plan to participate and compete in trials, however, you need more specialized training.

Effectively communicating with your dog requires a close connection and proper training. A good trainer will emphasize the dog's individuality and know what motivates him. Pictured is the author's oldest son, Vincent Renna.

Consistency is the most important element of training. Using too many trainers, for example, can be confusing for you and your dog. Try to find an experienced trainer with whom you are comfortable, and stick with it if you are seeing the results you want. Experienced trainers realize that no two dogs are alike and are able to bring out the best in each dog they work with. Each dog needs individual attention and has specific needs. An experienced trainer will help your dog reach his full potential. Experienced trainers can also teach you how to communicate with your dog in a way that makes sense to him. The experienced trainer will make sure you understand what is required of you to communicate with your dog in a clear, concise manner.

Lessons may be private or semiprivate. In either format, lessons are usually conducted as several short sessions interspersed with rest periods. During the rest breaks, the owner can learn by watching other dogs being trained. By sticking to a regular schedule, you should see steady progress. You should be able to tell pretty quickly if you feel comfortable with the

An experienced, fearless herding dog is invaluable to a stockman, as this English Shepherd winningly demonstrates.

instructor, if the physical setup is conducive to teaching the dog, and if the instructor knows what he or she is doing.

Sponsoring Clubs

There are several organizations in the United States that offer herding tests and competition for all herding breeds. The levels of competition and titles available differ from one organization to the next. Further, there are noncompetitive levels offered by each club that are designed to assess a dog's instinctive herding ability.

American Kennel Club

AKC herding events are open to any AKC-registered dog. Participants can earn one of two noncompetitive titles: Herding Tested (HT) and Pre-Trial Tested (PT). These are scored on a pass/fail basis. To qualify for the HT title, a dog must receive two passing scores under two different testers. The dog must demonstrate natural ability and desire to keep the stock together in a group and attempt to control their movement. At the conclusion of the test, the dog must stop at the handler's direction followed by a recall.

AKC herding tests provide opportunities for pet dogs, like this Bearded Collie, to discover and display their herding dog roots.

Herding Started (HS), Herding Intermediate (HI), and Herding Advanced (HX) titles are awarded in competitive classes. Dogs meet the criteria for titles by earning three qualifying scores under three different judges. When an HX is attained, the dog is eligible to compete for a Herding Championship certificate (HCH). The HCH certificate is awarded to dogs that have earned a total of fifteen points in advanced classes by finishing first through fourth place based on the number of dogs competing in the class, with no less than two first place wins.

The AKC offers three different courses. Course A is considered an all-around farm or ranch type course. Course B was designed after open field trials similar to those used in the ISDS, and Course C is a boundary-style course where dogs herd a flock of at least twenty sheep to different unfenced areas; over a bridge, across a road, and so on.

American Herding Breed Association

The AHBA offers herding tests and a trial program. Both levels of tests, Herding Capability Tested (HCT) and Junior Herding Dog (JHD), are judged on a pass/fail basis. The HCT and the JHD titles both require two passing scores under different testers.

The first "leg" of the HCT does not require formal training. The dog must demonstrate natural herding instincts and desire to keep stock grouped together and try to manage their movement. The second leg of the HCT requires that in addition to keeping stock grouped together, the dog must move the stock in a controlled fashion from one end of a pen to the other and demonstrate a stop and a recall.

To earn the JHD title, a dog must demonstrate his ability to collect and control stock, move stock in straight lines and turns, negotiate obstacles, and make a reliable stop on command at the re-pen.

Australian Shepherd Club of America

ASCA trials are open to all herding breeds. Dogs are graded on the

Professional working dogs and pet dogs alike revel in the excitement of working with livestock and doing the job they were born to do.

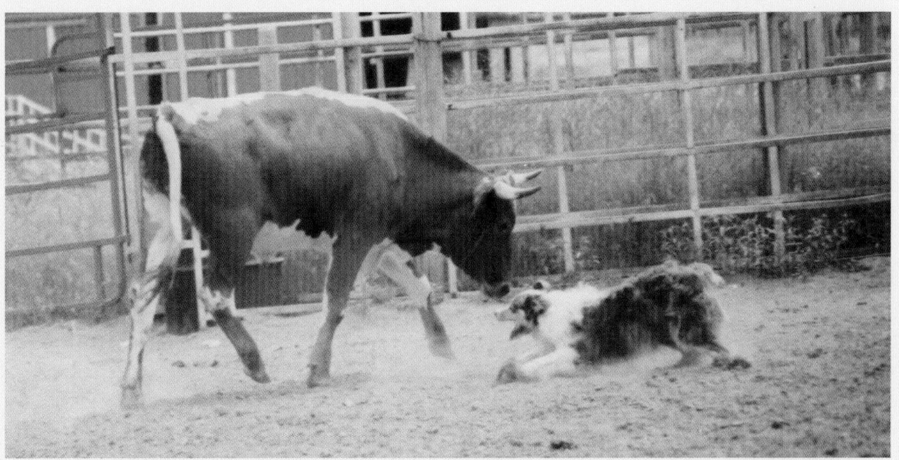

No bull, indeed! Australian Shepherds exhibit their prowess in working all kinds of livestock, including this giant bovine brute.

manner and degree of efficiency that they display while they herd a small group (three to ten animals) of livestock through an obstacle course and back to be penned.

Started Trial Dog (STD), Open Trial Dog (OTD), Advanced Trial Dog (ATD), or Post Advanced Trial Dog (PATD) certification is awarded to any dog earning two qualifying scores in each division and class of stock under two different judges. The class of stock the title was received in is noted at the end of the title. For example ATD-c indicates the ATD was earned in the cattle division. Once dogs meet the criteria for an ATD in a specific class of stock, they are eligible to compete in Post Advanced Division, an optional division for sheep and cattle.

Certification on each class of stock (cattle, sheep, or ducks) must be earned, in order, from Started through Advanced. Dogs that have earned an Advanced level degree in all three classes of stock are entitled to a Working Trial Championship (WTCH).

ASCA also has a noncompetitive Ranch Dog Program designed to recognize dogs that earn their keep by assisting their owners in a stock-related situation (stockyards, auctions, and rodeos).

Enjoying the good life, this baby Bouvier des Flandres radiates all the signs of health and vitality.

Chapter 7

Health Care and Treating Injuries

Keeping your herding dog healthy can be done by providing proper nutrition. A balanced diet directly affects your dog's skin and coat, weight, energy level. Feeding your dog a healthy diet and providing him with plenty of exercise will keep him healthy and feeling his best.

Preparing for the First Veterinary Visit

At between seven and sixteen weeks of age, your puppy goes through an important developmental stage. This is the time when puppies learn (whether we teach them or not!) which things in life are good and which are not. This developmental stage used to be called a "fear period" by many behaviorists because during this period many animals develop lifelong fears. Now commonly referred to as a critical socialization or developmental stage, this is a rare window of opportunity for us to teach puppies to become confident, psychologically healthy dogs.

Unfortunately, this is the same time period during which puppies receive their first examination and vaccinations from your veterinarian. Many puppies learn to be afraid of the veterinary office and staff at this time, and some puppies actually will learn to growl or bite during subsequent visits.

Dogs not properly trained for veterinary care can be difficult to handle, scared, and traumatized. Even such routine procedures as vaccinations, spaying or neutering, teeth cleaning, and checkups can be very stressful for dogs, and by extension for their owners. They can be stressful for veterinarians and their staffs as well: veterinarians do not like handling uncooperative and aggressive dogs.

You can prepare your dog for his first checkup by practicing certain things at home. For instance, practice looking inside his ears and mouth. You can play with his paws so he'll be less jumpy when others examine his feet and trim his nails. You can also socialize your dog to behave around other animals.

Then drive with your dog to the parking lot of the veterinary clinic. Park the car but remain inside. Play with or food-reward the dog in the car for a while, and then drive home. Drive to the parking lot again, and this time take the dog out of the car. Walk the dog around the lot and play with or food-reward the dog for a while. When the dog seems relaxed (and not anxious about entering the clinic), take the dog home.

At a later date, with your vet's approval, bring your dog inside the clinic without an appointment, arrange for a staff member to give your dog a favorite treat, and then take him home.

Finally, at your first scheduled vet visit, keep an eye on your dog as well as others. Talk to your dog and keep him relaxed with lots of praise and rewards. Belly rubs are ideal. Bring your dog's favorite toys and treats with you. You will be amazed by the results of these desensitization techniques.

Throughout a dog's life, even the healthiest of dogs will visit the vet several times for regular physical checkups and booster shots. Prepare your dog early and your experience at the veterinary hospital will be less stressful, whether you are there for a routine checkup or a sudden emergency.

Drug Sensitivity

Certain herding breeds may be hypersensitive to certain drugs. Breeds with known hypersensitivity include Australian Shepherds, Collies, German Shepherd Dogs, McNabs, Old English Sheepdogs, Shetland Sheepdogs, and a variety of mixed herding breeds.

A wide range of drugs may provoke hypersensitivity reactions,

The amount of exercise that a working sheepdog needs is provided on the job.

In Season

If your bitch comes into season and you choose not to breed her, you can safely give her two capfuls of liquid chlorophyll (available at most health-supplement shops) as soon as she comes into heat. The chlorophyll masks the odor and will take the stress off the male animals during this time. The chlorophyll can be discontinued at the end of the heat cycle.

including antibiotics, cancer drugs, steroids, heart medications, and antiparasitic agents. The drug Ivermectin, also known as Avermectin, used to prevent heartworm, has killed dogs that are sensitive to it. Imodium (Loperamide), an over-the-counter antidiarrheal agent, and Metronidazole, commonly prescribed to treat Giardia, are also associated with canine hypersensitivity.

This reaction is due to a genetic mutation known as multiple drug resistance (MDR1). The barrier (P-glycoprotein) that protects the brain by transporting a variety of drugs from the brain tissues back into the capillaries does not function properly. It causes dangerous neurological effects, including death.

You can learn more about the MDR1 defect and get the latest information on drug sensitivity or find out how to get your dog tested for MDR1 sensitivity by visiting www.vetmed.wsu.edu/depts-VCPL or by contacting the Veterinary Clinical Pharmacology Laboratory at Washington State University College of Veterinary Medicine, PO Box 609, Pullman, WA 99165-0609 (phone/fax: 509-335-3745) or VCPL@vetmed.wsu.edu.

Unless your dog has been tested and found to be free from the MDR1 mutation, it is a good idea to print a list of the drugs that have been documented or strongly suspected to cause problems and give them to your vet to keep in your dog's medical file.

First Aid at Home

First keep the emergency phone numbers, both during and after business hours, of your vet handy, along with the address and hours of your veterinary clinic and a backup urgent care clinic. Next assemble the following basic supplies: scissors, blanket, gauze pads, cloth strips to be used as bandages, rectal thermometer, tweezers, hydrogen peroxide, antibiotic ointment, instant cold packs, rags, eye wash, and a muzzle or material to make a muzzle out of should one become necessary. An injured dog may bite when in pain, even if he has never bitten before. Be very cautious when handling an injured animal, and know how to properly muzzle your dog, for your safety and his.

Dehydration is not uncommon for working dogs who live in hot, arid places. This hardworking Kelpie approaches his charges in the heat of the Australian sun.

Dehydration

Many herding activities around the country take place in the summer months. Large dogs, especially if they haven't shed their winter coats, may have difficulty dissipating excess heat during summer months while working stock. Your dog may retreat to a shady spot and show no interest in sheep. Provide plenty of cool water. Seek veterinary assistance if the dog's temperature rises above 102°F.

Herding dogs working on ranches or farms are more likely to become dehydrated than city dogs are, due to the nature of their working environments. Controlling the stock in the heat of the summer sun is physically very demanding. Herding dogs can easily become overheated by running from one side of the stock to the other side to keep them under control. In these working situations, the herding dog is continually on the move.

This is why it is so important to keep your herding dog well hydrated. You know how thirsty you get sitting out in the hot summer sun. Now try running for a few hours, and you'll see what I mean.

Usually, dehydration in a herding dog is caused by a combination of exposure to heat and lack of water. It is always a serious problem. If you suspect that your dog is dehydrated, get him some water immediately, and then get him to the veterinarian. Signs of dehydration can include a lack of elasticity to the skin, dry and sunken eyes, and a dry mouth and nose.

Dehydrated dogs will also experience a delay in capillary refill time. To test for this delay, gently pull the dog's lip away from his gum, and press a finger against the gum until the area whitens. When you release your finger, the color should return to the area almost immediately. A delay could be an indication of dehydration.

Dehydration must be addressed immediately; left untreated, it can cause multiple health problems, including organ failure and death. It is much easier for a working dog to become dehydrated than most other breeds, as working dogs spend many, many hours in the hot summer sun.

Check your dog's pulse in the groin area. Place your fingers on the inside of the hind leg until your fingers touch the abdomen, and gently move around until you feel the pulse. The pulse should be strong. Count the number of pulses in fifteen seconds and multiply that number by four. This will give you the beats per minute.

If your dog's breathing is labored, he vomits, or he has a high temperature (above the normal range of 100–102.5°F), he may collapse. If he does, wrap a cool soaking-wet towel around him, or put him into a bathtub or a tub of water until the rectal temperature is between 100 and 102°F. Take your dog to the vet immediately, as he may require fluids to be given intravenously.

Lots of water is the best way to replace fluids and avoid dehydration in the first place, but a severely dehydrated dog should not be allowed to take in large amounts at once. This will result in vomiting and a further loss of fluids. Let your dog drink small amounts over a period of time. Pedialyte used to rehydrate babies and children can be used also for dogs.

Injuries

There are a number of steps you can take to tend to an injured dog before taking him to the veterinarian for complete treatment. This section addresses the most common actions you may need to take.

Muzzling an Injured Dog

Working dogs are susceptible to injury, some minor, some quite serious. Most injuries should be handled by a vet. Injured dogs should wear a muzzle to protect the vet and anyone else handling the dog from being bitten. For this reason, it is important to get your dog comfortable wearing a muzzle.

It is important to know how to muzzle an injured dog. Care must be taken when handling weak or injured pets. Even gentle dogs might bite when they are in pain. In the event you do not have a muzzle on hand for an emergency, use a strip of soft cloth, rope, nylon pantyhose, or a necktie. Wrap it under the chin and tie behind the ears. Allow the pet to pant after handling by loosening or removing the muzzle.

The very first introduction to a muzzle should be a positive experience. Try this with a basket muzzle. Introduce the muzzle by showing it to your dog, and keep your voice very happy and upbeat. Let the dog sniff it, and praise him. Rub some peanut butter inside the muzzle or squirt some spray cheese on the inside and have your dog just lick it off without actually putting it on or strapping it over his face. Bacon strips and beef jerky also fit through the basket muzzle, and dogs love to eat them. Make sure to take the muzzle on and off several times over several days. Keep each experience positive, and eventually your dog will become accustomed to wearing a muzzle.

Cage or basket muzzles are the safest. Cloth muzzles are easy to find and may be a good choice for your first aid kit, as they do not take up a lot of room. Keep in mind when using a cloth muzzle that a dog may bite it with his front teeth or remove it by scratching at it with his paws. The cage or basket muzzle is more heavy-duty and not so easy to bite or get out of.

Some types of muzzles can be purchased from pet stores. Most pet stores do not carry basket or cage muzzles. You can usually find these muzzles in pet catalogs.

Controlling Bleeding

Apply firm, direct pressure to the source of the bleeding until the bleeding stops. Maintain the pressure for at least ten minutes (continually releasing the pressure to check the wound will hamper the clotting). Avoid bandages that cut off circulation. Keep the animal as

Laxatives

Laxatives are used to quickly expel plant material from the intestines. Mineral oil is safe and effective. Give one teaspoon for small dogs that weigh less than 25 pounds, one tablespoon to medium-size dogs 35–50 pounds, and two tablespoons to large or giant dogs, 50–100 pounds.

warm and quiet as possible. Get to your vet right away for treatment.

Dislocations

A dislocation is the painful misalignment of a bone from its joint. A dog with a dislocated knee or shoulder will not be able to walk. Don't try any amateur bone setting—get the dog to the vet as quickly as you can.

Head Injuries

When a dog gets kicked in the head, look for signs that his teeth and jaw are misaligned. Check for blood from the mouth and nose and for drooling. Your dog may not be able to close his mouth. Breathing may be difficult due to swelling in the back of the mouth and a bloody nose. Your pet may go into shock or lose consciousness.

If your dog is unconscious, make sure his head is lower than his body and his nose is pointed downward. This will prevent blood from the mouth or nose entering the lungs.

If he is conscious, do not attempt to support the jaw unless the jaw is hanging awkwardly and distressing the dog. In young dogs, the back of the mouth may be so swollen that the jaw needs to hang open to allow him to breathe properly. Get the dog to your vet right away.

Ear Injuries

Ear tips can be damaged by a glancing kick from either a cow or a horse. This type of injury is notorious for bleeding, and bleeding, and bleeding. Even when the bleeding finally stops, a dog need only shake his head to dislodge the clot and start the bleeding again. Clean the wound with warm salty water and apply pressure to both sides of the ear with a clean rag to stop the flow. Seek veterinary advice if the wound is deep or needs stitches.

Dogs working on the open range or on a ranch occasionally get foreign objects such as grass awns or insects in their ears. Suspect ear problems if you see your dog shaking his head or pawing at his ear. You may notice the dog holding the affected ear lower than the nonaffected ear. He may cry or yelp when the ear is rubbed. Do not attempt to probe the ear; rather, seek immediate veterinary advice. A veterinary examination is needed to extract a foreign body or diagnose an infection in the canal and to make sure the eardrum is intact. If the eardrum has ruptured, the condition is far more serious.

Eye Injuries

Eye injuries require prompt veterinary attention. Working dogs' eyes occasionally get kicked or cut by plant material, such as a seed, or scratched by a twig from low bushes. Symptoms of a foreign object in your dog's eye can be squinting or a spasm of the eyelid(s). Other signs are rubbing or pawing at his eye(s). You may notice discharge, redness, or a very small pupil. To treat the eye, gently open the eye to examine it. If the foreign object is loose, it may be washed out. To do this, tilt the animal's head upward and draw the lids apart. This may dislodge the object. Wash the eye with a gentle stream of clean water or saline (salty water). To make the saline solution, use one teaspoon of table salt to one pint of water. Boiled water (make sure to cool before using) is recommended because it will sterilize the solution. Human eye drops or saline used for cleaning contact lenses are both OK to use. Always use sterile water to clean and treat the eye. If the eye becomes infected, bandage the dog's front paw on the same side as the affected eye. This will help keep your dog from doing more damage to his injured eye.

Direct blows to the eye or head from a horse or cow could cause

The larger the livestock, the more common the injuries. Hulking creatures like cows and bulls threaten head and body harm.

bloody discharge in the white of the eye. Prolapses of the eye occur when the globe is forced outside the lids. This is a very serious injury, but prompt treatment by your veterinarian improves the chance of saving the eye. If there is to be any delay in reaching your veterinarian, the eye must be kept moist. Apply a cloth moistened with saline over the eye, then bandage it in place, wrapping around the jaw and, if necessary, the opposite ear to keep the bandage from slipping.

In the event of a kick to the head, the dog may also suffer a bloody nose. Tilt the head down so that the blood runs out of the nose and not down the back of the throat. Apply cold damp towels on the forehead and around the back of the neck.

Eye injuries can occur when a dog is down low, nipping at massive hocks and hooves.

This Vallhund may be scolding his big brown equine mate about potential dangers on the ranch.

Fractures

Fractures can be caused by a kick from a horse, cow, or other large animal. The obvious sign of a fracture is your dog's inability to walk on his limb, especially if his limb is pointing at an odd angle or appears to be deformed, twisted, or shortened. To treat a fracture, first gently lay the animal on a board, wooden door, or tarp padded with blankets so you can carry him without causing more damage.

If the dog is bleeding, stop the bleeding and watch for shock. Shock is the result of pain and/or blood loss. Severe blood loss can result from femoral or pelvic fractures. Try to control bleeding without causing more injury. Do not try to set the fracture. Pulling on the limb may cause more damage. Transport the pet to the veterinarian immediately,

Herding dogs are generally rugged, sturdy animals, and starting with a well-bred puppy is the best first step to having a healthy, hardy adult. This Aussie youngster is pictured with the author's husband, Vince.

supporting the injured part as best you can. Sometimes pain at or near the fracture site in some animals will not allow the limb to be handled at all. You should put a muzzle on the dog, as even good-natured dogs may bite when in pain.

Closed fractures do not break the skin. In an open fracture, the broken bone pierces the skin and is exposed. Open fractures are more serious, as infection may result, and veterinary care is essential for successful healing.

Lacerations

If your dog gets cut, the first thing you will need to do in caring for a wound is to stop the bleeding. This can be done by putting a cloth over the area and applying pressure. After the bleeding has stopped, clean the wound with hydrogen peroxide to prevent infection. Let the hydrogen peroxide sit for a few seconds, then flush the wound with warm water. Depending on the severity and the depth of the wound, you may need to see a vet for sutures.

It's not a pretty job, but someone's got to do it! This photo by Jeff Jaquish is titled "True Grit."

Toxic Substances

Below is a list of common household products that are toxic to dogs. These are common substances that most people have in their homes. If by chance your pet ingests any of the following, call the vet immediately. This is what to look for and how to initially treat your dog for poisoning until you get further instructions from a veterinarian.

Ammonia
Signs: Vomiting blood, abdominal pain, skin blisters, and burns.
Treatment: Wash skin with water and vinegar, give water mixed with small amount of vinegar, or you may give three egg whites orally.

Antifreeze
Signs: Vomiting, coma, kidney failure, death.
Treatment: Further induce vomiting, then administer one ounce of vodka orally followed by water.

Bleach
Signs: Burns of skin and mouth, vomiting.
Treatment: Further induce vomiting, give three egg whites orally.

Charcoal lighter fluid
Signs: Vomiting, breathing distress, shock, coma, or seizures.
Treatment: Further induce vomiting.

Detergents/Soap
Signs: Vomiting.
Treatment: Further induce vomiting, give three egg whites or milk orally, watch breathing.

Furniture polish
Signs: Vomiting, breathing distress, shock, coma, or seizures.
Treatments: Further induce vomiting, give laxatives.

Gasoline
Signs: Skin irritation, weakness, dementia, dilated pupils, vomiting, twitching.
Treatment: Further induce vomiting, give vegetable oil orally to block absorption, get into fresh air.

Ibuprofen
Signs: Vomiting, stomach ulceration, kidney failure.
Treatment: Further induce vomiting, give laxatives.

Insecticides

Signs: Excessive drooling, weakness, seizures, vomiting, dilated pupils.
Treatment: Wash off insecticide, administer atropine sulfate as the antidote.

Kerosene

Signs: Vomiting, breathing distress, shock, coma, or seizures.
Treatment: Further induce vomiting, give laxatives, give vegetable oil orally to block absorption.

Paint thinner

Signs: Vomiting, breathing distress, shock, coma, or seizures.
Treatment: Further induce vomiting, give laxatives.

Rat poison

Signs: Excess bleeding, anemia, cyanosis.
Treatment: Induce vomiting, requires vitamin K injections.

Rubbing alcohol

Signs: Weakness, lack of coordination, blindness, coma, dilated pupils, vomiting, and diarrhea.
Treatment: Further induce vomiting; give baking soda in water to neutralize acidosis.

Turpentine

Signs: Vomiting, diarrhea, bloody urine, neurological disorientation, coma, breathing distress.
Treatment: Further induce vomiting, give vegetable oil by mouth to block absorption, give laxatives.

Tylenol

Signs: Depression, fast heart rate, brown urine, anemia.
Treatment: Induce vomiting; give 500 milligrams vitamin C per twenty-five pounds of dog weight, followed by baking soda in water.

Note: How to Induce Vomiting
Give several teaspoons (for small and medium dogs) or several tablespoons (for large and giant dogs) of hydrogen peroxide orally. Repeat as needed to stimulate vomiting.

Another remedy: Use one teaspoon (for small and medium dogs) or one tablespoon (for large and giant dogs) of syrup of ipecac. Allow the dog to drink one cup of water as this will hasten the vomiting. Repeat as needed.

Teamwork—Little Wolf and Poco work together to convince an obstinate ram to return to the flock.

Acknowledgments

I dedicate this book to my husband, Vince, for his gracious support and patience during the long hours it took to produce this book. I appreciate his willingness to read the manuscript and spend much time offering his valuable advice.

I am especially thankful for my sister Jeanne Joy Taylor for helping me make my dream come true. I am grateful for her encouragement and help with the research.

I thank my family for their love and support.

A special thanks to Andrew DePrisco, editor-in-chief, and Kennel Club Books for taking on this project.

About the Author

Christine Hartnagle Renna grew up on a Colorado ranch in the heart of the Rocky Mountains, where her family used Australian Shepherds in their daily work. She currently resides in Broomfield, Colorado, with her husband, Vince, and two Australian Shepherds. She has two grown sons, Vincent and Jason.

Christine has a rich understanding of how dogs work and enjoys their keen ability to do more than one job. In her early years, she assisted her father, Ernest Hartnagle, in training one of their foundation stud dogs, Hud, in search-and-rescue. As a young teenager, she showed her beautiful Australian Shepherd Ch. Las Rocosa Sadie Blue CD to the distinction of becoming the first champion female Aussie of Colorado.

Christine, along with her family, developed the now famous Hartnagle Las Rocosa bloodlines, and as a result the kennel became the first to be admitted into the Australian Shepherd Club of America (ASCA) Hall of Fame for breeding a standard of excellence.

In her early twenties, Chris became a professional ballroom dance teacher for Fred Astaire Dancing Studios, where she met her husband. While raising two children, she competed in herding trials and has used herding dogs to round up and bring in sheep from the open prairie on her parents' ranch in Kiowa, Colorado. For Chris, herding dogs have always been a way of life and she wouldn't have it any other way. She not only appreciates their herding instincts but also loves their loyalty, companionship, and smarts.

Index